Stree... ad.
Britain's clearest street mapping for miles.
WEST YORKSHIRE
WIGAN
TYNE & WEAR
DERBY, LEICESTER NOTTINGHAM
CHESHIRE
BLACKPOOL PRESTON
CARDIFF NEWPORT
BRISTOL, BATH
BRADFORD-ON-AVON, CLEVEDON, PORTISHEAD, TROWBRIDGE, WESTON-SUPER-MARE, YATE
AA Street by Street
ESSEX
GREATER MANCHESTER
HAMPSHIRE
SUSSEX
PLUS HASLEMERE
ROYAL TUNBRIDGE
AA Street by Street
NEW EDITION
LONDON
Extended Coverage of the Capital
BRITAIN'S CLEAREST STREET MAPPING
Quick and easy to navigate from page-to-page
Car parks, one-way streets and petrol stations clearly marked
AA recommended pubs and hotels
"The most practical, clear and easy to use."
Street by Street maps & atlases
Britain's largest travel publisher
Order online at www.theAA.com/travel
AA

AA

Theory Test

The official questions and answers for car drivers

AA Publishing

Produced by AA Publishing.

First edition 1996
Reprinted 1996 (5 times)
Second edition with revised questions 1997
Reprinted 1998 (twice)
Third edition with revised questions 1998
Reprinted with amendments 1998 (twice)
Fourth edition with revised questions 1999
Reprinted 2000
Fifth edition with revised questions 2000
Sixth edition with revised questions 2001
Reprinted 2002 (twice) and June 2002 with amendment
Seventh edition with revised questions 2003.
Reprinted with amendments 2005
Eighth edition with revised questions 2005
Ninth edition with revised questions 2006
Reprinted 2006 (twice)

ISBN-10: 0-7495-5010-4
ISBN-13: 978-0-7495-5010-3

Published by AA Publishing (a trading name of Automobile Association Developments Limited, whose registered office is Fanum House, Basing View, Basingstoke, Hampshire RG21 4EA; registered number 1878835).
A03182

A CIP catalogue record for this book is available from the British Library.

Colour separation by Keenes.
Printed in Spain by Graficas Estella.

While every effort has been made to include the widest possible range of questions available at the time of printing, the Government may from time to time change, add or remove questions, and the publisher cannot be held responsible for questions that may appear on a question paper which were not available for inclusion in this book.

Contents

Introduction

The Theory Test

You have to pass two driving tests before you can apply for a full driving licence. The Theory Test was introduced in 1996 to check that drivers know more than just how to operate a car. This book contains the official car questions from the Driving Standards Agency (DSA) that you may have to answer. You will have to pass both the question part and the new video Hazard Perception part to pass your Theory Test, before you can apply for the Practical Test.

The Theory Test consists of 35 questions, and a separate video clips section, called Hazard Perception. You will have 40 minutes to complete the question part of the test, using a touch-screen, and all questions are multiple-choice. You have to score 30 out of 35 on the theory questions to pass. The Government may, from time to time, introduce new or amended questions. However, if you are fully prepared on each topic, you will be in a position to answer any question.

How to use this book

This book contains all the official questions for car drivers which appear in the question bank of the Driving Standards Agency (DSA). You could be tested on any of these questions when you take your touch-screen Theory Test.

The questions in this book are arranged in themes, such as Safety Margins and Hazard Awareness. Each theme has its own colour band, to help you find your way around. However, it is not cut and dried, and as you start to work through the questions you will soon discover that similar questions on the same topic may appear in different theme sections. Don't be put off by this, but read each question and the choice of answers very carefully. A similar question may be being asked in a different way, in order to test your full understanding.

You'll find all the answers to the questions at the back of the book. That way, you can easily test yourself to see what you are getting right, and what you need to work on.

Questions marked with an **NI** symbol are those not found in Theory Test papers in Northern Ireland.

How to study for the Theory Test

Remember

- Do not try too many questions at once.
- Do not try to learn the answers by heart.
- The order of the questions in this book may be different from how they are arranged in the actual test – so do not try to memorise the order.

How to answer the questions

Each questions has four, five or six answers. You must mark the boxes with the correct answer or answers. Each question tells you how many answers to mark.

Study each question carefully, making sure you understand what it is asking you. Look carefully at any diagram, drawing or photograph. Before you look at the answers given, decide what you think the right answer may be. You can then select the answer that matches the one you had decided on. If you follow this system, you will avoid being confused by answers that appear to be similar.

Hazard Perception

The video clips element of the Theory Test is known as Hazard Perception. Its aim is to find out how good you are at noticing hazards developing on the road ahead. The test will also show how much you know about the risks of driving, that is, risks to you as a driver, risks to your passengers and risks to other road users.

The test lasts for about 20 minutes. First you will be given some instructions explaining how it works; you will also get a chance to practise with the computer and mouse before you start the test 'for real'. This is to make sure you know what to expect on the test, and that you are happy with what you have to do.

Next you will see film or video clips of real street scenes with traffic such as motor vehicles, pedestrians, cyclists, etc. The scenes are shot from the point of view of a driver in a car. You have to notice hazards that are developing on the road ahead – that is, problems that could lead to an accident. As soon as you notice a hazard developing, click on the mouse control. You will

have plenty of time to see the hazard, but the sooner you notice it, the more marks you will score.

Every clip has at least one hazard in it – some clips may have more than one hazard. You currently have to score 44 out of 75 to pass **but** the pass mark may change and it is advisable to check with your driving instructor or the Driving Standards Agency before sitting your test. (Note that the computer has checks built in to show up anyone trying to cheat – for example, someone who keeps clicking the mouse all the time!)

All the film clips have been shot on 'real roads' and contain all sorts of hazards. However, you will only score points for 'developing' hazards.

For each hazard you spot you get one or more points. The more quickly you spot the hazard developing on-screen, and click on it with the mouse, the higher your score. But be aware that each test clip will only be shown once. You will not have an opportunity to go back to an earlier clip and change your response, so you need to concentrate.

Remember, you have to pass both the theory questions and hazard perception to pass the Theory Test. At the end of the test they will tell you your scores for both parts. Even if you only failed on one part of the Theory Test, you still have to take both parts again next time.

Preparing for Hazard Perception

Learner drivers need more training in how to spot hazards, because they are often so busy thinking about using the car's controls that they forget to watch the road and traffic. Learner drivers, and new drivers are up to two seconds slower at spotting hazards than more experienced drivers. Proper training can really help you to see more of the hazards that you will meet when driving, and to see those hazards earlier. So you're less likely to have an accident.

A hazard is anything that might cause you to change speed or direction when driving. The Hazard Perception element of the Theory Test is about spotting developing hazards. This is one of the key skills of good driving, and is also called anticipation. Anticipating hazards, such as car doors opening or children running into the road, means looking out for them in advance and taking the appropriate action now.

As you get more driving experience you will start to learn about times and places where you are most likely to meet hazards. An example of this is the rush hour. You know that people take more risks when driving in the rush hour. Maybe they have to drop their children off at school before going to work. Maybe they are late for a business meeting or are in a hurry to get home. So you have to be prepared for bad driving, for example, other drivers pulling out in front of you.

Much of *The Highway Code* is about the hazards you find at junctions. You might be on a minor road and have to turn out on to a major road where you can't see clearly both ways; or you might be at a crossroads where there are no signs saying which vehicle has priority (should go first).

Your driving instructor has been trained to help you learn hazard perception skills, and can give you plenty of practice in what to look out for when driving, how to anticipate hazards, and what action to take when you have to deal with hazards of all kinds. You won't be able to practise with the real video clips used in the test, of course, but training books and practice videos will be made available.

Preparing for both tests

You are strongly recommended to prepare for the Theory Test at the same time as you develop your skills behind the wheel for the Practical Test. Obviously, there are many similarities between the two tests – it is all about helping to make you a safer driver on today's busy roads. By preparing for both tests at the same time, you will reinforce your knowledge and understanding of all aspects of driving and you will improve your chances of passing both tests first time.

Selecting a driving school

When you select a driving school to teach you the practical skills, make sure they are prepared to advise and help you with the Theory Test. Good driving schools will provide theory practice papers for you to complete before you take the real test. These papers will help you judge your level of knowledge and help with your preparation. Check with friends who have been taught recently, and make sure you understand the difference between an instructor who displays a pink badge or licence (a trainee instructor) and one who displays a green badge or licence (a fully qualified instructor).

Price is important, so find out whether the school offers any discounts for blocks or courses of lessons paid in advance; if you decide to pay in advance, make sure the driving school is reputable. If lesson prices are very low, ask yourself 'why?' Check how long the lesson will last, as some driving schools offer lessons of less than 60 minutes. And don't forget to ask about the car you'll be learning to drive in. Is it modern and reliable? Is it insured? Does it have dual controls?

As with all courses, there are a number of subjects you will need to master. All good driving schools will have available a progress sheet and syllabus, which sets out all the skills you will need and keeps a record of your progress. You will probably find that if you take a two-hour lesson every week, your rate of progress will surprise you!

It is important that you should not take your Theory Test too early in your course of practical lessons. This is because you need the experience of meeting real hazards while you are learning to drive, so that you will be able to pass the Hazard Perception part of the Theory Test. You must pass the Theory Test before you can take the Practical Test. Agree a plan of action with your driving instructor.

After a few hours of driving tuition the instructor will discuss with you a structured course to suit your needs and you can agree on the likely date when you will be ready to take the Practical Test. Once you have passed your Theory Test, you can apply for a Practical Test appointment; this will give you added incentive to prepare thoroughly.

AA driving school

The AA has a driving school that only uses fully qualified instructors, who are all familiar with the Theory Test, Hazard Perception and the Practical Test. Why not give them a try? You can ring for details on freephone 0800 60 70 80 or visit the website at **www.AAdrivingschool.co.uk**

Being a good driver is more than just having the knowledge and the skills – it is about applying them with the right attitude. No one is a 'natural' or a 'perfect' driver. All drivers make mistakes. Being careful, courteous and considerate to other road users will complement the skills and knowledge you will acquire in the coming weeks and make you a good and safe driver.

Further information

For lots of hints and tips on driving or to take a mock Theory Test visit **www.AAdrivingschool.co.uk**

1 **Before you make a U-turn in the road, you should**

Mark one answer

- ☐ **A.** give an arm signal as well as using your indicators
- ☐ **B.** signal so that other drivers can slow down for you
- ☐ **C.** look over your shoulder for a final check
- ☐ **D.** select a higher gear than normal

2 **As you approach this bridge you should**

Mark three answers

- ☐ **A.** move into the middle of the road to get a better view
- ☐ **B.** slow down
- ☐ **C.** get over the bridge as quickly as possible
- ☐ **D.** consider using your horn
- ☐ **E.** find another route
- ☐ **F.** beware of pedestrians

3 **When following a large vehicle you should keep well back because this**

Mark one answer

- ☐ **A.** allows you to corner more quickly
- ☐ **B.** helps the large vehicle to stop more easily
- ☐ **C.** allows the driver to see you in the mirrors
- ☐ **D.** helps you to keep out of the wind

4 **In which of these situations should you avoid overtaking?**

Mark one answer

- ☐ **A.** Just after a bend
- ☐ **B.** In a one-way street
- ☐ **C.** On a 30mph road
- ☐ **D.** Approaching a dip in the road

5 **This road marking warns**

Mark one answer

- ☐ **A.** drivers to use the hard shoulder
- ☐ **B.** overtaking drivers there is a bend to the left
- ☐ **C.** overtaking drivers to move back to the left
- ☐ **D.** drivers that it is safe to overtake

6 **Your mobile phone rings while you are travelling. You should**

Mark one answer

- ☐ **A.** stop immediately
- ☐ **B.** answer it immediately
- ☐ **C.** pull up in a suitable place
- ☐ **D.** pull up at the nearest kerb

7 Why are these yellow lines painted across the road?

Mark one answer

- ☐ **A.** To help you choose the correct lane
- ☐ **B.** To help you keep the correct separation distance
- ☐ **C.** To make you aware of your speed
- ☐ **D.** To tell you the distance to the roundabout

8 You are approaching traffic lights that have been on green for some time. You should

Mark one answer

- ☐ **A.** accelerate hard
- ☐ **B.** maintain your speed
- ☐ **C.** be ready to stop
- ☐ **D.** brake hard

9 Which of the following should you do before stopping?

Mark one answer

- ☐ **A.** Sound the horn
- ☐ **B.** Use the mirrors
- ☐ **C.** Select a higher gear
- ☐ **D.** Flash your headlights

10 What does the term 'blind spot' mean for a driver?

Mark one answer

- ☐ **A.** An area covered by your right-hand mirror
- ☐ **B.** An area not covered by your headlights
- ☐ **C.** An area covered by your left-hand mirror
- ☐ **D.** An area not covered by your mirrors

11 Objects hanging from your interior mirror may

Mark two answers

- ☐ **A.** restrict your view
- ☐ **B.** improve your driving
- ☐ **C.** distract your attention
- ☐ **D.** help your concentration

12 Which of the following may cause loss of concentration on a long journey?

Mark four answers

- ☐ **A.** Loud music
- ☐ **B.** Arguing with a passenger
- ☐ **C.** Using a mobile phone
- ☐ **D.** Putting in a cassette tape
- ☐ **E.** Stopping regularly to rest
- ☐ **F.** Pulling up to tune the radio

13 On a long motorway journey boredom can cause you to feel sleepy. You should

Mark two answers

- ☐ **A.** leave the motorway and find a safe place to stop
- ☐ **B.** keep looking around at the surrounding landscape
- ☐ **C.** drive faster to complete your journey sooner
- ☐ **D.** ensure a supply of fresh air into your vehicle
- ☐ **E.** stop on the hard shoulder for a rest

14 You are driving at dusk. You should switch your lights on

Mark two answers

- ☐ **A.** even when street lights are not lit
- ☐ **B.** so others can see you
- ☐ **C.** only when others have done so
- ☐ **D.** only when street lights are lit

15 You are most likely to lose concentration when driving if you

Mark two answers

- ☐ **A.** use a mobile phone
- ☐ **B.** listen to very loud music
- ☐ **C.** switch on the heated rear window
- ☐ **D.** look at the door mirrors

16 Which FOUR are most likely to cause you to lose concentration while you are driving?

Mark four answers

- ☐ **A.** Using a mobile phone
- ☐ **B.** Talking into a microphone
- ☐ **C.** Tuning your car radio
- ☐ **D.** Looking at a map
- ☐ **E.** Checking the mirrors
- ☐ **F.** Using the demisters

17 You should not use a mobile phone while driving

Mark one answer

- ☐ **A.** until you are satisfied that no other traffic is near
- ☐ **B.** unless you are able to drive one-handed
- ☐ **C.** because it might distract your attention from the road ahead
- ☐ **D.** because reception is poor when the engine is running

18 Your vehicle is fitted with a hands-free phone system. Using this equipment whilst driving

Mark one answer

- ☐ **A.** is quite safe as long as you slow down
- ☐ **B.** could distract your attention from the road
- ☐ **C.** is recommended by *The Highway Code*
- ☐ **D.** could be very good for road safety

19 Using a hands-free phone is likely to

Mark one answer

- ☐ **A.** improve your safety
- ☐ **B.** increase your concentration
- ☐ **C.** reduce your view
- ☐ **D.** divert your attention

20 You should ONLY use a mobile phone when

Mark one answer

- ☐ **A.** receiving a call
- ☐ **B.** suitably parked
- ☐ **C.** driving at less than 30mph
- ☐ **D.** driving an automatic vehicle

21 Using a mobile phone while you are driving

Mark one answer

- ☐ **A.** is acceptable in a vehicle with power steering
- ☐ **B.** will reduce your field of vision
- ☐ **C.** could distract your attention from the road
- ☐ **D.** will affect your vehicle's electronic systems

22 What is the safest way to use a mobile phone in your vehicle?

Mark one answer

- [ ] **A.** Use hands-free equipment
- [ ] **B.** Find a suitable place to stop
- [ ] **C.** Drive slowly on a quiet road
- [ ] **D.** Direct your call through the operator

23 You are driving on a wet road. You have to stop your vehicle in an emergency. You should

Mark one answer

- [ ] **A.** apply the handbrake and footbrake together
- [ ] **B.** keep both hands on the wheel
- [ ] **C.** select reverse gear
- [ ] **D.** give an arm signal

24 When you are moving off from behind a parked car you should

Mark three answers

- [ ] **A.** look round before you move off
- [ ] **B.** use all the mirrors on the vehicle
- [ ] **C.** look round after moving off
- [ ] **D.** use the exterior mirrors only
- [ ] **E.** give a signal if necessary
- [ ] **F.** give a signal after moving off

25 You are travelling along this narrow country road. When passing the cyclist you should go

Mark one answer

- [ ] **A.** slowly, sounding the horn as you pass
- [ ] **B.** quickly, leaving plenty of room
- [ ] **C.** slowly, leaving plenty of room
- [ ] **D.** quickly, sounding the horn as you pass

26 Your vehicle is fitted with a hand-held telephone. To use the telephone you should

Mark one answer

- [ ] **A.** reduce your speed
- [ ] **B.** find a safe place to stop
- [ ] **C.** steer the vehicle with one hand
- [ ] **D.** be particularly careful at junctions

27 To answer a call on your mobile phone while travelling you should

Mark one answer

- [ ] **A.** reduce your speed wherever you are
- [ ] **B.** stop in a proper and convenient place
- [ ] **C.** keep the call time to a minimum
- [ ] **D.** slow down and allow others to overtake

28 **Your mobile phone rings while you are on the motorway. Before answering you should**

Mark one answer

- ☐ **A.** reduce your speed to 30mph
- ☐ **B.** pull up on the hard shoulder
- ☐ **C.** move into the left-hand lane
- ☐ **D.** stop in a safe place

29 **You are turning right onto a dual carriageway. What should you do before emerging?**

Mark one answer

- ☐ **A.** Stop, apply the handbrake and then select a low gear
- ☐ **B.** Position your vehicle well to the left of the side road
- ☐ **C.** Check that the central reservation is wide enough for your vehicle
- ☐ **D.** Make sure that you leave enough room for a vehicle behind

30 **You lose your way on a busy road. What is the best action to take?**

Mark one answer

- ☐ **A.** Stop at traffic lights and ask pedestrians
- ☐ **B.** Shout to other drivers to ask them the way
- ☐ **C.** Turn into a side road, stop and check a map
- ☐ **D.** Check a map, and keep going with the traffic flow

31 **You are waiting to emerge from a junction. The windscreen pillar is restricting your view. What should you be particularly aware of?**

Mark one answer

- ☐ **A.** Lorries
- ☐ **B.** Buses
- ☐ **C.** Motorcyclists
- ☐ **D.** Coaches

32 **When emerging from junctions which is most likely to obstruct your view?**

Mark one answer

- ☐ **A.** Windscreen pillars
- ☐ **B.** Steering wheel
- ☐ **C.** Interior mirror
- ☐ **D.** Windscreen wipers

33 **Windscreen pillars can obstruct your view. You should take particular care when**

Mark one answer

- ☐ **A.** driving on a motorway
- ☐ **B.** driving on a dual carriageway
- ☐ **C.** approaching a one-way street
- ☐ **D.** approaching bends and junctions

34 **You cannot see clearly behind when reversing. What should you do?**

Mark one answer

- ☐ **A.** Open your window to look behind
- ☐ **B.** Open the door and look behind
- ☐ **C.** Look in the nearside mirror
- ☐ **D.** Ask someone to guide you

35 When you see a hazard ahead you should use the mirrors. Why is this?

Mark one answer

- A. Because you will need to accelerate out of danger
- B. To assess how your actions will affect following traffic
- C. Because you will need to brake sharply to a stop
- D. To check what is happening on the road ahead

36 You are waiting to turn right at the end of a road. Your view is obstructed by parked vehicles. What should you do?

Mark one answer

- A. Stop and then move forward slowly and carefully for a proper view
- B. Move quickly to where you can see so you only block traffic from one direction
- C. Wait for a pedestrian to let you know when it is safe for you to emerge
- D. Turn your vehicle around immediately and find another junction to use

37 Your vehicle is fitted with a navigation system. How should you avoid letting this distract you while driving?

Mark one answer

- A. Keep going and input your destination into the system
- B. Keep going as the system will adjust to your route
- C. Stop immediately to view and use the system
- D. Stop in a safe place before using the system

38 Using a mobile phone when driving is illegal. The chance of you having an accident while using one is

Mark one answer

- A. two times higher
- B. four times higher
- C. six times higher
- D. ten times higher

39 You are driving on a motorway and want to use your mobile phone. What should you do?

Mark one answer

- A. Try to find a safe place on the hard shoulder
- B. Leave the motorway and stop in a safe place
- C. Use the next exit and pull up on the slip road
- D. Move to the left lane and reduce your speed

40 Using a mobile phone when driving is illegal. Your chances of having an accident increases by

Mark one answer

- A. two times
- B. four times
- C. eight times
- D. twelve times

41 Using a mobile phone when driving is illegal. If you do so your chances of having an accident increase by how many times?

Mark one answer

- A. two
- B. four
- C. ten
- D. twenty

42 At a pelican crossing the flashing amber light means you MUST

Mark one answer

- [ ] **A.** stop and wait for the green light
- [ ] **B.** stop and wait for the red light
- [ ] **C.** give way to pedestrians waiting to cross
- [ ] **D.** give way to pedestrians already on the crossing

43 You should never wave people across at pedestrian crossings because

Mark one answer

- [ ] **A.** there may be another vehicle coming
- [ ] **B.** they may not be looking
- [ ] **C.** it is safer for you to carry on
- [ ] **D.** they may not be ready to cross

44 At a puffin crossing, which colour follows the green signal?

Mark one answer

- [ ] **A.** Steady red
- [ ] **B.** Flashing amber
- [ ] **C.** Steady amber
- [ ] **D.** Flashing green

45 The conditions are good and dry. You could use the 'two-second rule'

Mark one answer

- [ ] **A.** before restarting the engine after it has stalled
- [ ] **B.** to keep a safe gap from the vehicle in front
- [ ] **C.** before using the 'Mirror-Signal-Manoeuvre' routine
- [ ] **D.** when emerging on wet roads

46 'Tailgating' means

Mark one answer

- [ ] **A.** using the rear door of a hatchback car
- [ ] **B.** reversing into a parking space
- [ ] **C.** following another vehicle too closely
- [ ] **D.** driving with rear fog lights on

47 Following this vehicle too closely is unwise because

Mark one answer

- [ ] **A.** your brakes will overheat
- [ ] **B.** your view ahead is increased
- [ ] **C.** your engine will overheat
- [ ] **D.** your view ahead is reduced

48 You are following a vehicle on a wet road. You should leave a time gap of at least

Mark one answer

- [ ] **A.** one second
- [ ] **B.** two seconds
- [ ] **C.** three seconds
- [ ] **D.** four seconds

49 You are in a line of traffic. The driver behind you is following very closely. What action should you take?

Mark one answer

- [ ] **A.** Ignore the following driver and continue to travel within the speed limit
- [ ] **B.** Slow down, gradually increasing the gap between you and the vehicle in front
- [ ] **C.** Signal left and wave the following driver past
- [ ] **D.** Move over to a position just left of the centre line of the road

50 A long, heavily laden lorry is taking a long time to overtake you. What should you do?

Mark one answer

- ☐ **A.** Speed up
- ☐ **B.** Slow down
- ☐ **C.** Hold your speed
- ☐ **D.** Change direction

51 Which of the following vehicles will use blue flashing beacons?

Mark three answers

- ☐ **A.** Motorway maintenance
- ☐ **B.** Bomb disposal
- ☐ **C.** Blood transfusion
- ☐ **D.** Police patrol
- ☐ **E.** Breakdown recovery

52 Which THREE of these emergency services might have blue flashing beacons?

Mark three answers

- ☐ **A.** Coastguard
- ☐ **B.** Bomb disposal
- ☐ **C.** Gritting lorries
- ☐ **D.** Animal ambulances
- ☐ **E.** Mountain rescue
- ☐ **F.** Doctors' cars

53 When being followed by an ambulance showing a flashing blue beacon you should

Mark one answer

- ☐ **A.** pull over as soon as safely possible to let it pass
- ☐ **B.** accelerate hard to get away from it
- ☐ **C.** maintain your speed and course
- ☐ **D.** brake harshly and immediately stop in the road

54 What type of emergency vehicle is fitted with a green flashing beacon?

Mark one answer

- ☐ **A.** Fire engine
- ☐ **B.** Road gritter
- ☐ **C.** Ambulance
- ☐ **D.** Doctor's car

55 A flashing green beacon on a vehicle means

Mark one answer

- ☐ **A.** police on non-urgent duties
- ☐ **B.** doctor on an emergency call
- ☐ **C.** road safety patrol operating
- ☐ **D.** gritting in progress

56 A vehicle has a flashing green beacon. What does this mean?

Mark one answer

- ☐ **A.** A doctor is answering an emergency call
- ☐ **B.** The vehicle is slow moving
- ☐ **C.** It is a motorway police patrol vehicle
- ☐ **D.** The vehicle is carrying hazardous chemicals

57 Diamond-shaped signs give instructions to

Mark one answer

- ☐ **A.** tram drivers
- ☐ **B.** bus drivers
- ☐ **C.** lorry drivers
- ☐ **D.** taxi drivers

58 On a road where trams operate, which of these vehicles will be most at risk from the tram rails?

Mark one answer

- ☐ **A.** Cars
- ☐ **B.** Cycles
- ☐ **C.** Buses
- ☐ **D.** Lorries

59 **What should you use your horn for?**

Mark one answer

- [ ] **A.** To alert others to your presence
- [ ] **B.** To allow you right of way
- [ ] **C.** To greet other road users
- [ ] **D.** To signal your annoyance

60 **You are in a one-way street and want to turn right. You should position yourself**

Mark one answer

- [ ] **A.** in the right-hand lane
- [ ] **B.** in the left-hand lane
- [ ] **C.** in either lane, depending on the traffic
- [ ] **D.** just left of the centre line

61 **You wish to turn right ahead. Why should you take up the correct position in good time?**

Mark one answer

- [ ] **A.** To allow other drivers to pull out in front of you
- [ ] **B.** To give a better view into the road that you're joining
- [ ] **C.** To help other road users know what you intend to do
- [ ] **D.** To allow drivers to pass you on the right

62 **At which type of crossing are cyclists allowed to ride across with pedestrians?**

Mark one answer

- [ ] **A.** Toucan
- [ ] **B.** Puffin
- [ ] **C.** Pelican
- [ ] **D.** Zebra

63 **A bus has stopped at a bus stop ahead of you. Its right-hand indicator is flashing. You should**

Mark one answer

- [ ] **A.** flash your headlights and slow down
- [ ] **B.** slow down and give way if it is safe to do so
- [ ] **C.** sound your horn and keep going
- [ ] **D.** slow down and then sound your horn

64 **You are travelling at the legal speed limit. A vehicle comes up quickly behind, flashing its headlights. You should**

Mark one answer

- [ ] **A.** accelerate to make a gap behind you
- [ ] **B.** touch the brakes sharply to show your brake lights
- [ ] **C.** maintain your speed to prevent the vehicle from overtaking
- [ ] **D.** allow the vehicle to overtake

65 **You should ONLY flash your headlights to other road users**

Mark one answer

- [ ] **A.** to show that you are giving way
- [ ] **B.** to show that you are about to turn
- [ ] **C.** to tell them that you have right of way
- [ ] **D.** to let them know that you are there

66 You are approaching unmarked crossroads. How should you deal with this type of junction?

Mark one answer

- [ ] **A.** Accelerate and keep to the middle
- [ ] **B.** Slow down and keep to the right
- [ ] **C.** Accelerate looking to the left
- [ ] **D.** Slow down and look both ways

67 You are approaching a pelican crossing. The amber light is flashing. You must

Mark one answer

- [ ] **A.** give way to pedestrians who are crossing
- [ ] **B.** encourage pedestrians to cross
- [ ] **C.** not move until the green light appears
- [ ] **D.** stop even if the crossing is clear

68 At puffin crossings, which light will not show to a driver?

Mark one answer

- [ ] **A.** Flashing amber
- [ ] **B.** Red
- [ ] **C.** Steady amber
- [ ] **D.** Green

69 You should leave at least a two-second gap between your vehicle and the one in front when conditions are

Mark one answer

- [ ] **A.** wet
- [ ] **B.** good
- [ ] **C.** damp
- [ ] **D.** foggy

70 You are driving on a clear night. There is a steady stream of oncoming traffic. The national speed limit applies. Which lights should you use?

Mark one answer

- [ ] **A.** Full beam headlights
- [ ] **B.** Sidelights
- [ ] **C.** Dipped headlights
- [ ] **D.** Fog lights

71 You are driving behind a large goods vehicle. It signals left but steers to the right. You should

Mark one answer

- [ ] **A.** slow down and let the vehicle turn
- [ ] **B.** drive on, keeping to the left
- [ ] **C.** overtake on the right of it
- [ ] **D.** hold your speed and sound your horn

72 You are driving along this road. The red van cuts in close in front of you. What should you do?

Mark one answer

- [ ] **A.** Accelerate to get closer to the red van
- [ ] **B.** Give a long blast on the horn
- [ ] **C.** Drop back to leave the correct separation distance
- [ ] **D.** Flash your headlights several times

73 **You are waiting in a traffic queue at night. To avoid dazzling following drivers you should**

Mark one answer
- [ ] **A.** apply the handbrake only
- [ ] **B.** apply the footbrake only
- [ ] **C.** switch off your headlights
- [ ] **D.** use both the handbrake and footbrake

74 **You are driving in traffic at the speed limit for the road. The driver behind is trying to overtake. You should**

Mark one answer
- [ ] **A.** move closer to the car ahead, so the driver behind has no room to overtake
- [ ] **B.** wave the driver behind to overtake when it is safe
- [ ] **C.** keep a steady course and allow the driver behind to overtake
- [ ] **D.** accelerate to get away from the driver behind

75 **You are driving at night on an unlit road behind another vehicle. You should**

Mark one answer
- [ ] **A.** flash your headlights
- [ ] **B.** use dipped beam headlights
- [ ] **C.** switch off your headlights
- [ ] **D.** use full beam headlights

76 **A bus lane on your left shows no times of operation. This means it is**

Mark one answer
- [ ] **A.** not in operation at all
- [ ] **B.** only in operation at peak times
- [ ] **C.** in operation 24 hours a day
- [ ] **D.** only in operation in daylight hours

77 **You are driving along a country road. A horse and rider are approaching. What should you do?**

Mark two answers
- [ ] **A.** Increase your speed
- [ ] **B.** Sound your horn
- [ ] **C.** Flash your headlights
- [ ] **D.** Drive slowly past
- [ ] **E.** Give plenty of room
- [ ] **F.** Rev your engine

78 A person herding sheep asks you to stop. You should

Mark one answer

- [ ] **A.** ignore them as they have no authority
- [ ] **B.** stop and switch off your engine
- [ ] **C.** continue on but drive slowly
- [ ] **D.** try and get past quickly

79 When overtaking a horse and rider you should

Mark one answer

- [ ] **A.** sound your horn as a warning
- [ ] **B.** go past as quickly as possible
- [ ] **C.** flash your headlights as a warning
- [ ] **D.** go past slowly and carefully

80 You are approaching a zebra crossing. Pedestrians are waiting to cross. You should

Mark one answer

- [ ] **A.** give way to the elderly and infirm only
- [ ] **B.** slow down and prepare to stop
- [ ] **C.** use your headlights to indicate they can cross
- [ ] **D.** wave at them to cross the road

81 You are driving a slow-moving vehicle on a narrow winding road. You should

Mark one answer

- [ ] **A.** keep well out to stop vehicles overtaking dangerously
- [ ] **B.** wave following vehicles past you if you think they can overtake quickly
- [ ] **C.** pull in safely when you can, to let following vehicles overtake
- [ ] **D.** give a left signal when it is safe for vehicles to overtake you

82 You have a loose filler cap on your diesel fuel tank. This will

Mark two answers

- [ ] **A.** waste fuel and money
- [ ] **B.** make roads slippery for other road users
- [ ] **C.** improve your vehicle's fuel consumption
- [ ] **D.** increase the level of exhaust emissions

83 To avoid spillage after refuelling, you should make sure that

Mark one answer

- [ ] **A.** your tank is only three-quarters full
- [ ] **B.** you have used a locking filler cap
- [ ] **C.** you check your fuel gauge is working
- [ ] **D.** your filler cap is securely fastened

84 A vehicle pulls out in front of you at a junction. What should you do?

Mark one answer

- [ ] **A.** Swerve past it and sound your horn
- [ ] **B.** Flash your headlights and drive up close behind
- [ ] **C.** Slow down and be ready to stop
- [ ] **D.** Accelerate past it immediately

85 You stop for pedestrians waiting to cross at a zebra crossing. They do not start to cross. What should you do?

Mark one answer

- [ ] **A.** Be patient and wait
- [ ] **B.** Sound your horn
- [ ] **C.** Carry on
- [ ] **D.** Wave them to cross

86 You are following this lorry. You should keep well back from it to

Mark one answer

- [ ] **A.** give you a good view of the road ahead
- [ ] **B.** stop following traffic from rushing through the junction
- [ ] **C.** prevent traffic behind you from overtaking
- [ ] **D.** allow you to hurry through the traffic lights if they change

87 You are approaching a red light at a puffin crossing. Pedestrians are on the crossing. The red light will stay on until

Mark one answer

- [ ] **A.** you start to edge forward on to the crossing
- [ ] **B.** the pedestrians have reached a safe position
- [ ] **C.** the pedestrians are clear of the front of your vehicle
- [ ] **D.** a driver from the opposite direction reaches the crossing

88 Which instrument panel warning light would show that headlights are on full beam?

Mark one answer

- [ ] **A.**

- [ ] **B.**

- [ ] **C.**

- [ ] **D.**

89 If your vehicle uses diesel fuel, take extra care when refuelling. Diesel fuel when spilt is

Mark one answer

- [ ] **A.** sticky
- [ ] **B.** odourless
- [ ] **C.** clear
- [ ] **D.** slippery

90 What style of driving causes increased risk to everyone?

Mark one answer

- [ ] **A.** Considerate
- [ ] **B.** Defensive
- [ ] **C.** Competitive
- [ ] **D.** Responsible

91 **Which of these, if allowed to get low, could cause an accident?**

Mark one answer

- [ ] **A.** Anti-freeze level
- [ ] **B.** Brake fluid level
- [ ] **C.** Battery water level
- [ ] **D.** Radiator coolant level

92 **Which TWO are badly affected if the tyres are under-inflated?**

Mark two answers

- [ ] **A.** Braking
- [ ] **B.** Steering
- [ ] **C.** Changing gear
- [ ] **D.** Parking

93 **Motor vehicles can harm the environment. This has resulted in**

Mark three answers

- [ ] **A.** air pollution
- [ ] **B.** damage to buildings
- [ ] **C.** less risk to health
- [ ] **D.** improved public transport
- [ ] **E.** less use of electrical vehicles
- [ ] **F.** using up of natural resources

94 **Excessive or uneven tyre wear can be caused by faults in which THREE of the following?**

Mark three answers

- [ ] **A.** The gearbox
- [ ] **B.** The braking system
- [ ] **C.** The accelerator
- [ ] **D.** The exhaust system
- [ ] **E.** Wheel alignment
- [ ] **F.** The suspension

95 **You must NOT sound your horn**

Mark one answer

- [ ] **A.** between 10pm and 6am in a built-up area
- [ ] **B.** at any time in a built-up area
- [ ] **C.** between 11.30pm and 7am in a built-up area
- [ ] **D.** between 11.30pm and 6am on any road

96 **The pictured vehicle is 'environmentally friendly' because it**

Mark three answers

- [ ] **A.** reduces noise pollution
- [ ] **B.** uses diesel fuel
- [ ] **C.** uses electricity
- [ ] **D.** uses unleaded fuel
- [ ] **E.** reduces parking spaces
- [ ] **F.** reduces town traffic

97 **Supertrams or Light Rapid Transit (LRT) systems are environmentally friendly because**

Mark one answer

- [ ] **A.** they use diesel power
- [ ] **B.** they use quieter roads
- [ ] **C.** they use electric power
- [ ] **D.** they do not operate during rush hour

98 **'Red routes' in major cities have been introduced to**

Mark one answer

- [ ] **A.** raise the speed limits
- [ ] **B.** help the traffic flow
- [ ] **C.** provide better parking
- [ ] **D.** allow lorries to load more freely

99 **Road humps, chicanes, and narrowings are**

Mark one answer

- [ ] **A.** always at major road works
- [ ] **B.** used to increase traffic speed
- [ ] **C.** at toll-bridge approaches only
- [ ] **D.** traffic calming measures

100 **The purpose of a catalytic converter is to reduce**

Mark one answer
- [ ] A. fuel consumption
- [ ] B. the risk of fire
- [ ] C. toxic exhaust gases
- [ ] D. engine wear

101 **Catalytic converters are fitted to make the**

Mark one answer
- [ ] A. engine produce more power
- [ ] B. exhaust system easier to replace
- [ ] C. engine run quietly
- [ ] D. exhaust fumes cleaner

102 **It is essential that tyre pressures are checked regularly. When should this be done?**

Mark one answer
- [ ] A. After any lengthy journey
- [ ] B. After travelling at high speed
- [ ] C. When tyres are hot
- [ ] D. When tyres are cold

103 **When should you NOT use your horn in a built-up area?**

Mark one answer
- [ ] A. Between 8pm and 8am
- [ ] B. Between 9pm and dawn
- [ ] C. Between dusk and 8am
- [ ] D. Between 11.30pm and 7am

104 **You will use more fuel if your tyres are**

Mark one answer
- [ ] A. under-inflated
- [ ] B. of different makes
- [ ] C. over-inflated
- [ ] D. new and hardly used

105 **How should you dispose of a used battery?**

Mark two answers
- [ ] A. Take it to a local authority site
- [ ] B. Put it in the dustbin
- [ ] C. Break it up into pieces
- [ ] D. Leave it on waste land
- [ ] E. Take it to a garage
- [ ] F. Burn it on a fire

106 **What is most likely to cause high fuel consumption?**

Mark one answer
- [ ] A. Poor steering control
- [ ] B. Accelerating around bends
- [ ] C. Staying in high gears
- [ ] D. Harsh braking and accelerating

107 **The fluid level in your battery is low. What should you top it up with?**

Mark one answer
- [ ] A. Battery acid
- [ ] B. Distilled water
- [ ] C. Engine oil
- [ ] D. Engine coolant

108 **You need to top up your battery. What level should you fill to?**

Mark one answer
- [ ] A. The top of the battery
- [ ] B. Half-way up the battery
- [ ] C. Just below the cell plates
- [ ] D. Just above the cell plates

109 **You have too much oil in your engine. What could this cause?**

Mark one answer
- [ ] A. Low oil pressure
- [ ] B. Engine overheating
- [ ] C. Chain wear
- [ ] D. Oil leaks

110 You are parking on a two-way road at night. The speed limit is 40mph. You should park on the

Mark one answer
- [ ] **A.** left with parking lights on
- [ ] **B.** left with no lights on
- [ ] **C.** right with parking lights on
- [ ] **D.** right with dipped headlights on

111 You are parked on the road at night. Where must you use parking lights?

Mark one answer
- [ ] **A.** Where there are continuous white lines in the middle of the road
- [ ] **B.** Where the speed limit exceeds 30mph
- [ ] **C.** Where you are facing oncoming traffic
- [ ] **D.** Where you are near a bus stop

112 Which FOUR of these must be in good working order for your car to be roadworthy?

Mark four answers
- [ ] **A.** The temperature gauge
- [ ] **B.** The speedometer
- [ ] **C.** The windscreen washers
- [ ] **D.** The windscreen wipers
- [ ] **E.** The oil warning light
- [ ] **F.** The horn

113 New petrol-engined cars must be fitted with catalytic converters. The reason for this is to

Mark one answer
- [ ] **A.** control exhaust noise levels
- [ ] **B.** prolong the life of the exhaust system
- [ ] **C.** allow the exhaust system to be recycled
- [ ] **D.** reduce harmful exhaust emissions

114 What can cause heavy steering?

Mark one answer
- [ ] **A.** Driving on ice
- [ ] **B.** Badly worn brakes
- [ ] **C.** Over-inflated tyres
- [ ] **D.** Under-inflated tyres

115 Driving with under-inflated tyres can affect

Mark two answers
- [ ] **A.** engine temperature
- [ ] **B.** fuel consumption
- [ ] **C.** braking
- [ ] **D.** oil pressure

116 Excessive or uneven tyre wear can be caused by faults in the

Mark two answers
- [ ] **A.** gearbox
- [ ] **B.** braking system
- [ ] **C.** suspension
- [ ] **D.** exhaust system

117 The main cause of brake fade is

Mark one answer
- [ ] **A.** the brakes overheating
- [ ] **B.** air in the brake fluid
- [ ] **C.** oil on the brakes
- [ ] **D.** the brakes out of adjustment

118 Your anti-lock brakes warning light stays on. You should

Mark one answer
- [ ] **A.** check the brake fluid level
- [ ] **B.** check the footbrake free play
- [ ] **C.** check that the handbrake is released
- [ ] **D.** have the brakes checked immediately

119 **While driving, this warning light on your dashboard comes on. It means**

Mark one answer

- [ ] **A.** a fault in the braking system
- [ ] **B.** the engine oil is low
- [ ] **C.** a rear light has failed
- [ ] **D.** your seat belt is not fastened

120 **It is important to wear suitable shoes when you are driving. Why is this?**

Mark one answer

- [ ] **A.** To prevent wear on the pedals
- [ ] **B.** To maintain control of the pedals
- [ ] **C.** To enable you to adjust your seat
- [ ] **D.** To enable you to walk for assistance if you break down

121 **The most important reason for having a properly adjusted head restraint is to**

Mark one answer

- [ ] **A.** make you more comfortable
- [ ] **B.** help you to avoid neck injury
- [ ] **C.** help you to relax
- [ ] **D.** help you to maintain your driving position

122 **What will reduce the risk of neck injury resulting from a collision?**

Mark one answer

- [ ] **A.** An air-sprung seat
- [ ] **B.** Anti-lock brakes
- [ ] **C.** A collapsible steering wheel
- [ ] **D.** A properly adjusted head restraint

123 **You are driving the children of a friend home from school. They are both under 14 years old. Who is responsible for making sure they wear a seat belt?**

Mark one answer

- [ ] **A.** An adult passenger
- [ ] **B.** The children
- [ ] **C.** You, the driver
- [ ] **D.** Your friend

124 **Car passengers MUST wear a seat belt if one is available, unless they are**

Mark one answer

- [ ] **A.** under 14 years old
- [ ] **B.** under 1.5 metres (5 feet) in height
- [ ] **C.** sitting in the rear seat
- [ ] **D.** exempt for medical reasons

125 **You are testing your suspension. You notice that your vehicle keeps bouncing when you press down on the front wing. What does this mean?**

Mark one answer

- [ ] **A.** Worn tyres
- [ ] **B.** Tyres under-inflated
- [ ] **C.** Steering wheel not located centrally
- [ ] **D.** Worn shock absorbers

126 **A roof rack fitted to your car will**

Mark one answer

- [ ] **A.** reduce fuel consumption
- [ ] **B.** improve the road handling
- [ ] **C.** make your car go faster
- [ ] **D.** increase fuel consumption

127 **It is illegal to drive with tyres that**

Mark one answer

- [ ] **A.** have been bought second-hand
- [ ] **B.** have a large deep cut in the side wall
- [ ] **C.** are of different makes
- [ ] **D.** are of different tread patterns

128 The legal minimum depth of tread for car tyres over three quarters of the breadth is

Mark one answer

- [ ] **A.** 1mm
- [ ] **B.** 1.6mm
- [ ] **C.** 2.5mm
- [ ] **D.** 4mm

129 You are carrying two 13-year-old children and their parents in your car. Who is responsible for seeing that the children wear seat belts?

Mark one answer

- [ ] **A.** The children's parents
- [ ] **B.** You, the driver
- [ ] **C.** The front-seat passenger
- [ ] **D.** The children

130 When a roof rack is not in use it should be removed. Why is this?

Mark one answer

- [ ] **A.** It will affect the suspension
- [ ] **B.** It is illegal
- [ ] **C.** It will affect your braking
- [ ] **D.** It will waste fuel

131 How can you, as a driver, help the environment?

Mark three answers

- [ ] **A.** By reducing your speed
- [ ] **B.** By gentle acceleration
- [ ] **C.** By using leaded fuel
- [ ] **D.** By driving faster
- [ ] **E.** By harsh acceleration
- [ ] **F.** By servicing your vehicle properly

132 To help the environment, you can avoid wasting fuel by

Mark three answers

- [ ] **A.** having your vehicle properly serviced
- [ ] **B.** making sure your tyres are correctly inflated
- [ ] **C.** not over-revving in the lower gears
- [ ] **D.** driving at higher speeds where possible
- [ ] **E.** keeping an empty roof rack properly fitted
- [ ] **F.** servicing your vehicle less regularly

133 To reduce the volume of traffic on the roads you could

Mark three answers

- [ ] **A.** use public transport more often
- [ ] **B.** share a car when possible
- [ ] **C.** walk or cycle on short journeys
- [ ] **D.** travel by car at all times
- [ ] **E.** use a car with a smaller engine
- [ ] **F.** drive in a bus lane

134 Which THREE of the following are most likely to waste fuel?

Mark three answers

- [ ] **A.** Reducing your speed
- [ ] **B.** Carrying unnecessary weight
- [ ] **C.** Using the wrong grade of fuel
- [ ] **D.** Under-inflated tyres
- [ ] **E.** Using different brands of fuel
- [ ] **F.** A fitted, empty roof rack

135 Which THREE things can you, as a road user, do to help the environment?

Mark three answers

- [ ] **A.** Cycle when possible
- [ ] **B.** Drive on under-inflated tyres
- [ ] **C.** Use the choke for as long as possible on a cold engine
- [ ] **D.** Have your vehicle properly tuned and serviced
- [ ] **E.** Watch the traffic and plan ahead
- [ ] **F.** Brake as late as possible without skidding

136 As a driver you can cause more damage to the environment by

Mark two answers
- A. choosing a fuel-efficient vehicle
- B. making a lot of short journeys
- C. driving in as high a gear as possible
- D. accelerating as quickly as possible
- E. having your vehicle regularly serviced

137 To help protect the environment you should NOT

Mark one answer
- A. remove your roof rack when unloaded
- B. use your car for very short journeys
- C. walk, cycle, or use public transport
- D. empty the boot of unnecessary weight

138 Which THREE does the law require you to keep in good condition?

Mark three answers
- A. Gears
- B. Transmission
- C. Headlights
- D. Windscreen
- E. Seat belts

139 Driving at 70mph uses more fuel than driving at 50mph by up to

Mark one answer
- A. 10%
- B. 30%
- C. 75%
- D. 100%

140 Your vehicle pulls to one side when braking. You should

Mark one answer
- A. change the tyres around
- B. consult your garage as soon as possible
- C. pump the pedal when braking
- D. use your handbrake at the same time

141 As a driver, you can help reduce pollution levels in town centres by

Mark one answer
- A. driving more quickly
- B. over-revving in a low gear
- C. walking or cycling
- D. driving short journeys

142 Unbalanced wheels on a car may cause

Mark one answer
- A. the steering to pull to one side
- B. the steering to vibrate
- C. the brakes to fail
- D. the tyres to deflate

143 Turning the steering wheel while your car is stationary can cause damage to the

Mark two answers
- A. gearbox
- B. engine
- C. brakes
- D. steering
- E. tyres

144 How can you reduce the chances of your car being broken into when leaving it unattended?

Mark one answer
- A. Take all valuables with you
- B. Park near a taxi rank
- C. Place any valuables on the floor
- D. Park near a fire station

145 You have to leave valuables in your car. It would be safer to

Mark one answer
- A. put them in a carrier bag
- B. park near a school entrance
- C. lock them out of sight
- D. park near a bus stop

146 How could you deter theft from your car when leaving it unattended?

Mark one answer

- A. Leave valuables in a carrier bag
- B. Lock valuables out of sight
- C. Put valuables on the seats
- D. Leave valuables on the floor

147 Which of the following may help to deter a thief from stealing your car?

Mark one answer

- A. Always keeping the headlights on
- B. Fitting reflective glass windows
- C. Always keeping the interior light on
- D. Etching the car number on the windows

148 How can you help to prevent your car radio being stolen?

Mark one answer

- A. Park in an unlit area
- B. Hide the radio with a blanket
- C. Park near a busy junction
- D. Install a security-coded radio

149 Which of the following should not be kept in your vehicle?

Mark one answer

- A. A first aid kit
- B. A road atlas
- C. The tax disc
- D. The vehicle documents

150 What should you do when leaving your vehicle?

Mark one answer

- A. Put valuable documents under the seats
- B. Remove all valuables
- C. Cover valuables with a blanket
- D. Leave the interior light on

151 You are parking your car. You have some valuables which you are unable to take with you. What should you do?

Mark one answer

- A. Park near a police station
- B. Put them under the driver's seat
- C. Lock them out of sight
- D. Park in an unlit side road

152 Which of these is most likely to deter the theft of your vehicle?

Mark one answer

- A. An immobiliser
- B. Tinted windows
- C. Locking wheel nuts
- D. A sun screen

153 Wherever possible, which one of the following should you do when parking at night?

Mark one answer

- A. Park in a quiet car park
- B. Park in a well-lit area
- C. Park facing against the flow of traffic
- D. Park next to a busy junction

154 When parking and leaving your car you should

Mark one answer

- A. park under a shady tree
- B. remove the tax disc
- C. park in a quiet road
- D. engage the steering lock

155 Rear-facing baby seats should NEVER be used on a seat protected with

Mark one answer

- A. an airbag
- B. seat belts
- C. head restraints
- D. seat covers

156 When leaving your vehicle parked and unattended you should

Mark one answer

- ☐ **A.** park near a busy junction
- ☐ **B.** park in a housing estate
- ☐ **C.** remove the key and lock it
- ☐ **D.** leave the left indicator on

157 How can you lessen the risk of your vehicle being broken into at night?

Mark one answer

- ☐ **A.** Leave it in a well-lit area
- ☐ **B.** Park in a quiet side road
- ☐ **C.** Don't engage the steering lock
- ☐ **D.** Park in a poorly-lit area

158 To help keep your car secure you could join a

Mark one answer

- ☐ **A.** vehicle breakdown organisation
- ☐ **B.** vehicle watch scheme
- ☐ **C.** advanced driver's scheme
- ☐ **D.** car maintenance class

159 Which TWO of the following will improve fuel consumption?

Mark two answers

- ☐ **A.** Reducing your road speed
- ☐ **B.** Planning well ahead
- ☐ **C.** Late and harsh braking
- ☐ **D.** Driving in lower gears
- ☐ **E.** Short journeys with a cold engine
- ☐ **F.** Rapid acceleration

160 You service your own vehicle. How should you get rid of the old engine oil?

Mark one answer

- ☐ **A.** Take it to a local authority site
- ☐ **B.** Pour it down a drain
- ☐ **C.** Tip it into a hole in the ground
- ☐ **D.** Put it into your dustbin

161 On a vehicle, where would you find a catalytic converter?

Mark one answer

- ☐ **A.** In the fuel tank
- ☐ **B.** In the air filter
- ☐ **C.** On the cooling system
- ☐ **D.** On the exhaust system

162 Why do MOT tests include a strict exhaust emission test?

Mark one answer

- ☐ **A.** To recover the cost of expensive garage equipment
- ☐ **B.** To help protect the environment against pollution
- ☐ **C.** To discover which fuel supplier is used the most
- ☐ **D.** To make sure diesel and petrol engines emit the same fumes

163 To reduce the damage your vehicle causes to the environment you should

Mark three answers

- ☐ **A.** use narrow side streets
- ☐ **B.** avoid harsh acceleration
- ☐ **C.** brake in good time
- ☐ **D.** anticipate well ahead
- ☐ **E.** use busy routes

164 Your vehicle has a catalytic converter. Its purpose is to reduce

Mark one answer

- ☐ **A.** exhaust noise
- ☐ **B.** fuel consumption
- ☐ **C.** exhaust emissions
- ☐ **D.** engine noise

165 A properly serviced vehicle will give

Mark two answers

- [ ] A. lower insurance premiums
- [ ] B. you a refund on your road tax
- [ ] C. better fuel economy
- [ ] D. cleaner exhaust emissions

166 You enter a road where there are road humps. What should you do?

Mark one answer

- [ ] A. Maintain a reduced speed throughout
- [ ] B. Accelerate quickly between each one
- [ ] C. Always keep to the maximum legal speed
- [ ] D. Drive slowly at school times only

167 When should you especially check the engine oil level?

Mark one answer

- [ ] A. Before a long journey
- [ ] B. When the engine is hot
- [ ] C. Early in the morning
- [ ] D. Every 6,000 miles

168 You are having difficulty finding a parking space in a busy town. You can see there is space on the zigzag lines of a zebra crossing. Can you park there?

Mark one answer

- [ ] A. No, unless you stay with your car
- [ ] B. Yes, in order to drop off a passenger
- [ ] C. Yes, if you do not block people from crossing
- [ ] D. No, not in any circumstances

169 When leaving your car unattended for a few minutes you should

Mark one answer

- [ ] A. leave the engine running
- [ ] B. switch the engine off but leave the key in
- [ ] C. lock it and remove the key
- [ ] D. park near a traffic warden

170 When parking and leaving your car for a few minutes you should

Mark one answer

- [ ] A. leave it unlocked
- [ ] B. lock it and remove the key
- [ ] C. leave the hazard warning lights on
- [ ] D. leave the interior light on

171 When leaving your car to help keep it secure you should

Mark one answer

- [ ] A. leave the hazard warning lights on
- [ ] B. lock it and remove the key
- [ ] C. park on a one-way street
- [ ] D. park in a residential area

172 When leaving your vehicle where should you park if possible?

Mark one answer

- [ ] A. Opposite a traffic island
- [ ] B. In a secure car park
- [ ] C. On a bend
- [ ] D. At or near a taxi rank

173 You are leaving your vehicle parked on a road. When may you leave the engine running?

Mark one answer

- [ ] A. If you will be parking for less than 5 minutes
- [ ] B. If the battery is flat
- [ ] C. When in a 20mph zone
- [ ] D. Never on any occasion

174 In which THREE places would parking your vehicle cause danger or obstruction to other road users?

Mark three answers

- [ ] **A.** In front of a property entrance
- [ ] **B.** At or near a bus stop
- [ ] **C.** On your driveway
- [ ] **D.** In a marked parking space
- [ ] **E.** On the approach to a level crossing

175 In which THREE places would parking cause an obstruction to others?

Mark three answers

- [ ] **A.** Near the brow of a hill
- [ ] **B.** In a lay-by
- [ ] **C.** Where the kerb is raised
- [ ] **D.** Where the kerb has been lowered for wheelchairs
- [ ] **E.** At or near a bus stop

176 You are away from home and have to park your vehicle overnight. Where should you leave it?

Mark one answer

- [ ] **A.** Opposite another parked vehicle
- [ ] **B.** In a quiet road
- [ ] **C.** Opposite a traffic island
- [ ] **D.** In a secure car park

177 Before starting a journey it is wise to plan your route. How can you do this?

Mark one answer

- [ ] **A.** Look at a map
- [ ] **B.** Contact your local garage
- [ ] **C.** Look in your vehicle handbook
- [ ] **D.** Check your vehicle registration document

178 It can help to plan your route before starting a journey. You can do this by contacting

Mark one answer **NI**

- [ ] **A.** your local filling station
- [ ] **B.** a motoring organisation
- [ ] **C.** the Driver Vehicle Licensing Agency
- [ ] **D.** your vehicle manufacturer

179 How can you plan your route before starting a long journey?

Mark one answer

- [ ] **A.** Check your vehicle's workshop manual
- [ ] **B.** Ask your local garage
- [ ] **C.** Use a route planner on the internet
- [ ] **D.** Consult your travel agents

180 Planning your route before setting out can be helpful. How can you do this?

Mark one answer

- [ ] **A.** Look in a motoring magazine
- [ ] **B.** Only visit places you know
- [ ] **C.** Try to travel at busy times
- [ ] **D.** Print or write down the route

181 Why is it a good idea to plan your journey to avoid busy times?

Mark one answer

- [ ] **A.** You will have an easier journey
- [ ] **B.** You will have a more stressful journey
- [ ] **C.** Your journey time will be longer
- [ ] **D.** It will cause more traffic congestion

182 Planning your journey to avoid busy times has a number of advantages. One of these is

Mark one answer

- [ ] **A.** your journey will take longer
- [ ] **B.** you will have a more pleasant journey
- [ ] **C.** you will cause more pollution
- [ ] **D.** your stress level will be greater

183 **It is a good idea to plan your journey to avoid busy times. This is because**

Mark one answer
- [ ] **A.** your vehicle will use more fuel
- [ ] **B.** you will see less road works
- [ ] **C.** it will help to ease congestion
- [ ] **D.** you will travel a much shorter distance

184 **By avoiding busy times when travelling**

Mark one answer
- [ ] **A.** you are more likely to be held up
- [ ] **B.** your journey time will be longer
- [ ] **C.** you will travel a much shorter distance
- [ ] **D.** you are less likely to be delayed

185 **It can help to plan your route before starting a journey. Why should you also plan an alternative route?**

Mark one answer
- [ ] **A.** Your original route may be blocked
- [ ] **B.** Your maps may have different scales
- [ ] **C.** You may find you have to pay a congestion charge
- [ ] **D.** Because you may get held up by a tractor

186 **You will find that driving smoothly can**

Mark one answer
- [ ] **A.** reduce journey times by about 15%
- [ ] **B.** increase fuel consumption by about 15%
- [ ] **C.** reduce fuel consumption by about 15%
- [ ] **D.** increase journey times by about 15%

187 **You can save fuel when conditions allow by**

Mark one answer
- [ ] **A.** using lower gears as often as possible
- [ ] **B.** accelerating sharply in each gear
- [ ] **C.** using each gear in turn
- [ ] **D.** missing out some gears

188 **As well as planning your route before starting a journey, you should also plan an alternative route. Why is this?**

Mark one answer
- [ ] **A.** To let another driver overtake
- [ ] **B.** Your first route may be blocked
- [ ] **C.** To avoid a railway level crossing
- [ ] **D.** In case you have to avoid emergency vehicles

189 **Who of these will not have to pay Congestion Charges in London?**

Mark one answer
- [ ] **A.** A van driver making deliveries
- [ ] **B.** A rider of a two-wheeled vehicle
- [ ] **C.** A car driver whose vehicle is more than 1000 cc
- [ ] **D.** A driver who just wants to park in the area

190 **Congestion Charges apply in the London area. Who of these will NOT have to pay?**

Mark one answer
- [ ] **A.** A person who lives in the area
- [ ] **B.** A driver making deliveries
- [ ] **C.** A person who is just driving through the area
- [ ] **D.** A driver with no other passengers in the vehicle

191 **You are making an appointment and will have to travel a long distance. You should**

Mark one answer
- [ ] **A.** allow plenty of time for your journey
- [ ] **B.** plan to go at busy times
- [ ] **C.** avoid all national speed limit roads
- [ ] **D.** prevent other drivers from overtaking

192 You are checking your trailer tyres. What is the legal minimum tread depth over the central three quarters of its breadth?

Mark one answer
- A. 1mm
- B. 1.6mm
- C. 2mm
- D. 2.6mm

193 How can driving in an Eco-safe manner help protect the environment?

Mark one answer
- A. Through the legal enforcement of speed regulations
- B. By increasing the number of cars on the road
- C. Through increased fuel bills
- D. By reducing exhaust emissions

194 What does Eco-safe driving achieve?

Mark one answer
- A. Increased fuel consumption
- B. Improved road safety
- C. Damage to the environment
- D. Increased exhaust emissions

195 How can missing out some gear changes save fuel?

Mark one answer
- A. By reducing the amount of time you are accelerating
- B. Because there is less need to use the footbrake
- C. By controlling the amount of steering
- D. Because coasting is kept to a minimum

196 Fuel consumption is at its highest when you are

Mark one answer
- A. braking
- B. coasting
- C. accelerating
- D. steering

197 Missing out some gears saves fuel by reducing the amount of time you spend

Mark one answer
- A. braking
- B. coasting
- C. steering
- D. accelerating

198 Rapid acceleration and heavy braking can lead to

Mark one answer
- A. reduced pollution
- B. increased fuel consumption
- C. reduced exhaust emissions
- D. increased road safety

199 What percentage of all emissions does road transport account for?

Mark one answer
- A. 10%
- B. 20%
- C. 30%
- D. 40%

200 Braking distances on ice can be

Mark one answer

- [ ] **A.** twice the normal distance
- [ ] **B.** five times the normal distance
- [ ] **C.** seven times the normal distance
- [ ] **D.** ten times the normal distance

201 Freezing conditions will affect the distance it takes you to come to a stop. You should expect stopping distances to increase by up to

Mark one answer

- [ ] **A.** two times
- [ ] **B.** three times
- [ ] **C.** five times
- [ ] **D.** ten times

202 In very hot weather the road surface can become soft. Which TWO of the following will be most affected?

Mark two answers

- [ ] **A.** The suspension
- [ ] **B.** The grip of the tyres
- [ ] **C.** The braking
- [ ] **D.** The exhaust

203 Where are you most likely to be affected by a side wind?

Mark one answer

- [ ] **A.** On a narrow country lane
- [ ] **B.** On an open stretch of road
- [ ] **C.** On a busy stretch of road
- [ ] **D.** On a long, straight road

204 In windy conditions you need to take extra care when

Mark one answer

- [ ] **A.** using the brakes
- [ ] **B.** making a hill start
- [ ] **C.** turning into a narrow road
- [ ] **D.** passing pedal cyclists

205 In good conditions, what is the typical stopping distance at 70mph?

Mark one answer

- [ ] **A.** 53 metres (175 feet)
- [ ] **B.** 60 metres (197 feet)
- [ ] **C.** 73 metres (240 feet)
- [ ] **D.** 96 metres (315 feet)

206 What is the shortest overall stopping distance on a dry road at 60mph?

Mark one answer

- [ ] **A.** 53 metres (175 feet)
- [ ] **B.** 58 metres (190 feet)
- [ ] **C.** 73 metres (240 feet)
- [ ] **D.** 96 metres (315 feet)

207 You are following a vehicle at a safe distance on a wet road. Another driver overtakes you and pulls into the gap you have left. What should you do?

Mark one answer

- [ ] **A.** Flash your headlights as a warning
- [ ] **B.** Try to overtake safely as soon as you can
- [ ] **C.** Drop back to regain a safe distance
- [ ] **D.** Stay close to the other vehicle until it moves on

208 When approaching a right-hand bend you should keep well to the left. Why is this?

Mark one answer

- [ ] **A.** To improve your view of the road
- [ ] **B.** To overcome the effect of the road's slope
- [ ] **C.** To let faster traffic from behind overtake
- [ ] **D.** To be positioned safely if you skid

209 You should not overtake when

Mark three answers

- [ ] **A.** intending to turn left shortly afterwards
- [ ] **B.** in a one-way street
- [ ] **C.** approaching a junction
- [ ] **D.** going up a long hill
- [ ] **E.** the view ahead is blocked

210 You have just gone through deep water. To dry off the brakes you should

Mark one answer

- [ ] **A.** accelerate and keep to a high speed for a short time
- [ ] **B.** go slowly while gently applying the brakes
- [ ] **C.** avoid using the brakes at all for a few miles
- [ ] **D.** stop for at least an hour to allow them time to dry

211 You are on a fast, open road in good conditions. For safety, the distance between you and the vehicle in front should be

Mark one answer

- [ ] **A.** a two-second time gap
- [ ] **B.** one car length
- [ ] **C.** 2 metres (6 feet 6 inches)
- [ ] **D.** two car lengths

212 What is the most common cause of skidding?

Mark one answer

- [ ] **A.** Worn tyres
- [ ] **B.** Driver error
- [ ] **C.** Other vehicles
- [ ] **D.** Pedestrians

213 You are driving on an icy road. How can you avoid wheelspin?

Mark one answer

- [ ] **A.** Drive at a slow speed in as high a gear as possible
- [ ] **B.** Use the handbrake if the wheels start to slip
- [ ] **C.** Brake gently and repeatedly
- [ ] **D.** Drive in a low gear at all times

214 Skidding is mainly caused by

Mark one answer

- [ ] **A.** the weather
- [ ] **B.** the driver
- [ ] **C.** the vehicle
- [ ] **D.** the road

215 You are driving in freezing conditions. What should you do when approaching a sharp bend?

Mark two answers

- [ ] **A.** Slow down before you reach the bend
- [ ] **B.** Gently apply your handbrake
- [ ] **C.** Firmly use your footbrake
- [ ] **D.** Coast into the bend
- [ ] **E.** Avoid sudden steering movements

216 You are turning left on a slippery road. The back of your vehicle slides to the right. You should

Mark one answer

- [ ] **A.** brake firmly and not turn the steering wheel
- [ ] **B.** steer carefully to the left
- [ ] **C.** steer carefully to the right
- [ ] **D.** brake firmly and steer to the left

217 You are braking on a wet road. Your vehicle begins to skid. It does not have anti-lock brakes. What is the FIRST thing you should do?

Mark one answer

- **A.** Quickly pull up the handbrake
- **B.** Release the footbrake fully
- **C.** Push harder on the brake pedal
- **D.** Gently use the accelerator

218 Travelling for long distances in neutral (known as coasting)

Mark one answer

- **A.** improves the driver's control
- **B.** makes steering easier
- **C.** reduces the driver's control
- **D.** uses more fuel

219 Before starting a journey in freezing weather you should clear ice and snow from your vehicle's

Mark four answers

- **A.** aerial
- **B.** windows
- **C.** bumper
- **D.** lights
- **E.** mirrors
- **F.** number plates

220 You are trying to move off on snow. You should use

Mark one answer

- **A.** the lowest gear you can
- **B.** the highest gear you can
- **C.** a high engine speed
- **D.** the handbrake and footbrake together

221 When driving in falling snow you should

Mark one answer

- **A.** brake firmly and quickly
- **B.** be ready to steer sharply
- **C.** use sidelights only
- **D.** brake gently in plenty of time

222 The main benefit of having four-wheel drive is to improve

Mark one answer

- **A.** road holding
- **B.** fuel consumption
- **C.** stopping distances
- **D.** passenger comfort

223 You are about to go down a steep hill. To control the speed of your vehicle you should

Mark one answer

- **A.** select a high gear and use the brakes carefully
- **B.** select a high gear and use the brakes firmly
- **C.** select a low gear and use the brakes carefully
- **D.** select a low gear and avoid using the brakes

224 How can you use your vehicle's engine as a brake?

Mark one answer

- **A.** By changing to a lower gear
- **B.** By selecting reverse gear
- **C.** By changing to a higher gear
- **D.** By selecting neutral gear

225 You wish to park facing DOWNHILL. Which TWO of the following should you do?

Mark two answers

- **A.** Turn the steering wheel towards the kerb
- **B.** Park close to the bumper of another car
- **C.** Park with two wheels on the kerb
- **D.** Put the handbrake on firmly
- **E.** Turn the steering wheel away from the kerb

226 **You are driving in a built-up area. You approach a speed hump. You should**

Mark one answer

- [ ] **A.** move across to the left-hand side of the road
- [ ] **B.** wait for any pedestrians to cross
- [ ] **C.** slow your vehicle right down
- [ ] **D.** stop and check both pavements

227 **You are on a long, downhill slope. What should you do to help control the speed of your vehicle?**

Mark one answer

- [ ] **A.** Select neutral
- [ ] **B.** Select a lower gear
- [ ] **C.** Grip the handbrake firmly
- [ ] **D.** Apply the parking brake gently

228 **Your vehicle is fitted with anti-lock brakes. To stop quickly in an emergency you should**

Mark one answer

- [ ] **A.** brake firmly and pump the brake pedal on and off
- [ ] **B.** brake rapidly and firmly without releasing the brake pedal
- [ ] **C.** brake gently and pump the brake pedal on and off
- [ ] **D.** brake rapidly once, and immediately release the brake pedal

229 **Anti-lock brakes prevent wheels from locking. This means the tyres are less likely to**

Mark one answer

- [ ] **A.** aquaplane
- [ ] **B.** skid
- [ ] **C.** puncture
- [ ] **D.** wear

230 **Anti-lock brakes reduce the chances of a skid occurring particularly when**

Mark one answer

- [ ] **A.** driving down steep hills
- [ ] **B.** braking during normal driving
- [ ] **C.** braking in an emergency
- [ ] **D.** driving on good road surfaces

231 **Anti-lock brakes are most effective when you**

Mark one answer

- [ ] **A.** keep pumping the footbrake to prevent skidding
- [ ] **B.** brake normally, but grip the steering wheel tightly
- [ ] **C.** brake promptly and firmly until you have slowed down
- [ ] **D.** apply the handbrake to reduce the stopping distance

232 **Your car is fitted with anti-lock brakes. You need to stop in an emergency. You should**

Mark one answer

- [ ] **A.** brake normally and avoid turning the steering wheel
- [ ] **B.** press the brake pedal promptly and firmly until you have stopped
- [ ] **C.** keep pushing and releasing the footbrake quickly to prevent skidding
- [ ] **D.** apply the handbrake to reduce the stopping distance

233 **Vehicles fitted with anti-lock brakes**

Mark one answer

- [ ] **A.** are impossible to skid
- [ ] **B.** can be steered while you are braking
- [ ] **C.** accelerate much faster
- [ ] **D.** are not fitted with a handbrake

234 Anti-lock brakes may not work as effectively if the road surface is

Mark two answers

- [ ] **A.** dry
- [ ] **B.** loose
- [ ] **C.** wet
- [ ] **D.** good
- [ ] **E.** firm

235 Anti-lock brakes are of most use when you are

Mark one answer

- [ ] **A.** braking gently
- [ ] **B.** driving on worn tyres
- [ ] **C.** braking excessively
- [ ] **D.** driving normally

236 Driving a vehicle fitted with anti-lock brakes allows you to

Mark one answer

- [ ] **A.** brake harder because it is impossible to skid
- [ ] **B.** drive at higher speeds
- [ ] **C.** steer and brake at the same time
- [ ] **D.** pay less attention to the road ahead

237 Anti-lock brakes can greatly assist with

Mark one answer

- [ ] **A.** a higher cruising speed
- [ ] **B.** steering control when braking
- [ ] **C.** control when accelerating
- [ ] **D.** motorway driving

238 When would an anti-lock braking system start to work?

Mark one answer

- [ ] **A.** After the parking brake has been applied
- [ ] **B.** Whenever pressure on the brake pedal is applied
- [ ] **C.** Just as the wheels are about to lock
- [ ] **D.** When the normal braking system fails to operate

239 You are driving a vehicle fitted with anti-lock brakes. You need to stop in an emergency. You should apply the footbrake

Mark one answer

- [ ] **A.** slowly and gently
- [ ] **B.** slowly but firmly
- [ ] **C.** rapidly and gently
- [ ] **D.** rapidly and firmly

240 Your vehicle has anti-lock brakes, but they may not always prevent skidding. This is most likely to happen when driving

Mark two answers

- [ ] **A.** in foggy conditions
- [ ] **B.** on surface water
- [ ] **C.** on loose road surfaces
- [ ] **D.** on dry tarmac
- [ ] **E.** at night on unlit roads

241 Anti-lock brakes will take effect when

Mark one answer

- [ ] **A.** you do not brake quickly enough
- [ ] **B.** maximum brake pressure has been applied
- [ ] **C.** you have not seen a hazard ahead
- [ ] **D.** speeding on slippery road surfaces

242 When driving in fog, which of the following are correct?

Mark three answers

- [ ] **A.** Use dipped headlights
- [ ] **B.** Use headlights on full beam
- [ ] **C.** Allow more time for your journey
- [ ] **D.** Keep close to the car in front
- [ ] **E.** Slow down
- [ ] **F.** Use sidelights only

243 You are driving along a country road. You see this sign. AFTER dealing safely with the hazard you should always

Mark one answer

- [ ] **A.** check your tyre pressures
- [ ] **B.** switch on your hazard warning lights
- [ ] **C.** accelerate briskly
- [ ] **D.** test your brakes

244 You are driving in heavy rain. Your steering suddenly becomes very light. You should

Mark one answer

- [ ] **A.** steer towards the side of the road
- [ ] **B.** apply gentle acceleration
- [ ] **C.** brake firmly to reduce speed
- [ ] **D.** ease off the accelerator

245 How can you tell when you are driving over black ice?

Mark one answer

- [ ] **A.** It is easier to brake
- [ ] **B.** The noise from your tyres sounds louder
- [ ] **C.** You will see tyre tracks on the road
- [ ] **D.** Your steering feels light

246 The roads are icy. You should drive slowly

Mark one answer

- [ ] **A.** in the highest gear possible
- [ ] **B.** in the lowest gear possible
- [ ] **C.** with the handbrake partly on
- [ ] **D.** with your left foot on the brake

247 You are driving along a wet road. How can you tell if your vehicle is aquaplaning?

Mark one answer

- [ ] **A.** The engine will stall
- [ ] **B.** The engine noise will increase
- [ ] **C.** The steering will feel very heavy
- [ ] **D.** The steering will feel very light

248 How can you tell if you are driving on ice?

Mark two answers

- [ ] **A.** The tyres make a rumbling noise
- [ ] **B.** The tyres make hardly any noise
- [ ] **C.** The steering becomes heavier
- [ ] **D.** The steering becomes lighter

249 You are driving along a wet road. How can you tell if your vehicle's tyres are losing their grip on the surface?

Mark one answer

- [ ] **A.** The engine will stall
- [ ] **B.** The steering will feel very heavy
- [ ] **C.** The engine noise will increase
- [ ] **D.** The steering will feel very light

250
You are travelling at 50mph on a good, dry road. What is your shortest overall stopping distance?

Mark one answer

- ☐ **A.** 36 metres (120 feet)
- ☐ **B.** 53 metres (175 feet)
- ☐ **C.** 75 metres (245 feet)
- ☐ **D.** 96 metres (315 feet)

251
Your overall stopping distance will be much longer when driving

Mark one answer

- ☐ **A.** in the rain
- ☐ **B.** in fog
- ☐ **C.** at night
- ☐ **D.** in strong winds

252
You have driven through a flood. What is the first thing you should do?

Mark one answer

- ☐ **A.** Stop and check the tyres
- ☐ **B.** Stop and dry the brakes
- ☐ **C.** Check your exhaust
- ☐ **D.** Test your brakes

253
You are on a good, dry road surface. Your vehicle has good brakes and tyres. What is the BRAKING distance at 50mph?

Mark one answer

- ☐ **A.** 38 metres (125 feet)
- ☐ **B.** 14 metres (46 feet)
- ☐ **C.** 24 metres (79 feet)
- ☐ **D.** 55 metres (180 feet)

254
You are on a good, dry road surface and your vehicle has good brakes and tyres. What is the typical overall STOPPING distance at 40mph?

Mark one answer

- ☐ **A.** 23 metres (75 feet)
- ☐ **B.** 36 metres (120 feet)
- ☐ **C.** 53 metres (175 feet)
- ☐ **D.** 96 metres (315 feet)

255
You are on a wet motorway with surface spray. You should use

Mark one answer

- ☐ **A.** hazard flashers
- ☐ **B.** dipped headlights
- ☐ **C.** rear fog lights
- ☐ **D.** sidelights

256 **You see this sign on the rear of a slow-moving lorry that you want to pass. It is travelling in the middle lane of a three-lane motorway. You should**

Mark one answer

- [ ] **A.** cautiously approach the lorry then pass on either side
- [ ] **B.** follow the lorry until you can leave the motorway
- [ ] **C.** wait on the hard shoulder until the lorry has stopped
- [ ] **D.** approach with care and keep to the left of the lorry

257 **Where would you expect to see these markers?**

Mark two answers

- [ ] **A.** On a motorway sign
- [ ] **B.** At the entrance to a narrow bridge
- [ ] **C.** On a large goods vehicle
- [ ] **D.** On a builder's skip placed on the road

258 **What does this signal from a police officer mean to oncoming traffic?**

Mark one answer

- [ ] **A.** Go ahead
- [ ] **B.** Stop
- [ ] **C.** Turn left
- [ ] **D.** Turn right

259 **What is the main hazard shown in this picture?**

Mark one answer

- [ ] **A.** Vehicles turning right
- [ ] **B.** Vehicles doing U-turns
- [ ] **C.** The cyclist crossing the road
- [ ] **D.** Parked cars around the corner

260 Which road user has caused a hazard?

Mark one answer

- ☐ **A.** The parked car (arrowed A)
- ☐ **B.** The pedestrian waiting to cross (arrowed B)
- ☐ **C.** The moving car (arrowed C)
- ☐ **D.** The car turning (arrowed D)

261 What should the driver of the car approaching the crossing do?

Mark one answer

- ☐ **A.** Continue at the same speed
- ☐ **B.** Sound the horn
- ☐ **C.** Drive through quickly
- ☐ **D.** Slow down and get ready to stop

262 What THREE things should the driver of the grey car (arrowed) be especially aware of?

Mark three answers

- ☐ **A.** Pedestrians stepping out between cars
- ☐ **B.** Other cars behind the grey car
- ☐ **C.** Doors opening on parked cars
- ☐ **D.** The bumpy road surface
- ☐ **E.** Cars leaving parking spaces
- ☐ **F.** Empty parking spaces

263 You think the driver of the vehicle in front has forgotten to cancel their right indicator. You should

Mark one answer

- ☐ **A.** flash your lights to alert the driver
- ☐ **B.** sound your horn before overtaking
- ☐ **C.** overtake on the left if there is room
- ☐ **D.** stay behind and not overtake

264 What is the main hazard the driver of the red car (arrowed) should be aware of?

Mark one answer

- [ ] **A.** Glare from the sun may affect the driver's vision
- [ ] **B.** The black car may stop suddenly
- [ ] **C.** The bus may move out into the road
- [ ] **D.** Oncoming vehicles will assume the driver is turning right

265 In heavy motorway traffic you are being followed closely by the vehicle behind. How can you lower the risk of an accident?

Mark one answer

- [ ] **A.** Increase your distance from the vehicle in front
- [ ] **B.** Tap your foot on the brake pedal sharply
- [ ] **C.** Switch on your hazard lights
- [ ] **D.** Move on to the hard shoulder and stop

266 You see this sign ahead. You should expect the road to

Mark one answer

- [ ] **A.** go steeply uphill
- [ ] **B.** go steeply downhill
- [ ] **C.** bend sharply to the left
- [ ] **D.** bend sharply to the right

267 You are approaching this cyclist. You should

Mark one answer

- [ ] **A.** overtake before the cyclist gets to the junction
- [ ] **B.** flash your headlights at the cyclist
- [ ] **C.** slow down and allow the cyclist to turn
- [ ] **D.** overtake the cyclist on the left-hand side

268 Why must you take extra care when turning right at this junction?

Mark one answer

- [ ] **A.** Road surface is poor
- [ ] **B.** Footpaths are narrow
- [ ] **C.** Road markings are faint
- [ ] **D.** There is reduced visibility

269 This yellow sign on a vehicle indicates this is

Mark one answer

- [ ] **A.** a broken-down vehicle
- [ ] **B.** a school bus
- [ ] **C.** an ice-cream van
- [ ] **D.** a private ambulance

270 When approaching this bridge you should give way to

Mark one answer

- [ ] **A.** bicycles
- [ ] **B.** buses
- [ ] **C.** motorcycles
- [ ] **D.** cars

271 What type of vehicle could you expect to meet in the middle of the road?

Mark one answer

- [ ] **A.** Lorry
- [ ] **B.** Bicycle
- [ ] **C.** Car
- [ ] **D.** Motorcycle

272 At this blind junction you must stop

Mark one answer

- [ ] **A.** behind the line, then edge forward to see clearly
- [ ] **B.** beyond the line at a point where you can see clearly
- [ ] **C.** only if there is traffic on the main road
- [ ] **D.** only if you are turning to the right

273 A driver pulls out of a side road in front of you. You have to brake hard. You should

Mark one answer

- [ ] **A.** ignore the error and stay calm
- [ ] **B.** flash your lights to show your annoyance
- [ ] **C.** sound your horn to show your annoyance
- [ ] **D.** overtake as soon as possible

274 An elderly person's driving ability could be affected because they may be unable to

Mark one answer

- [ ] **A.** obtain car insurance
- [ ] **B.** understand road signs
- [ ] **C.** react very quickly
- [ ] **D.** give signals correctly

275 You have just passed these warning lights. What hazard would you expect to see next?

Mark one answer

- [ ] **A.** A level crossing with no barrier
- [ ] **B.** An ambulance station
- [ ] **C.** A school crossing patrol
- [ ] **D.** An opening bridge

276 Why should you be especially cautious when going past this bus?

Mark two answers

- [ ] **A.** There is traffic approaching in the distance
- [ ] **B.** The driver may open the door
- [ ] **C.** It may suddenly move off
- [ ] **D.** People may cross the road in front of it
- [ ] **E.** There are bicycles parked on the pavement

277 In areas where there are 'traffic calming' measures you should

Mark one answer

- [ ] **A.** travel at a reduced speed
- [ ] **B.** always travel at the speed limit
- [ ] **C.** position in the centre of the road
- [ ] **D.** only slow down if pedestrians are near

278 You are planning a long journey. Do you need to plan rest stops?

Mark one answer

- ☐ **A.** Yes, you should plan to stop every half an hour
- ☐ **B.** Yes, regular stops help concentration
- ☐ **C.** No, you will be less tired if you get there as soon as possible
- ☐ **D.** No, only fuel stops will be needed

279 A driver does something that upsets you. You should

Mark one answer

- ☐ **A.** try not to react
- ☐ **B.** let them know how you feel
- ☐ **C.** flash your headlights several times
- ☐ **D.** sound your horn

280 The red lights are flashing. What should you do when approaching this level crossing?

Mark one answer

- ☐ **A.** Go through quickly
- ☐ **B.** Go through carefully
- ☐ **C.** Stop before the barrier
- ☐ **D.** Switch on hazard warning lights

281 What TWO main hazards should you be aware of when going along this street?

Mark two answers

- ☐ **A.** Glare from the sun
- ☐ **B.** Car doors opening suddenly
- ☐ **C.** Lack of road markings
- ☐ **D.** The headlights on parked cars being switched on
- ☐ **E.** Large goods vehicles
- ☐ **F.** Children running out from between vehicles

282 What is the main hazard you should be aware of when following this cyclist?

Mark one answer

- ☐ **A.** The cyclist may move to the left and dismount
- ☐ **B.** The cyclist may swerve out into the road
- ☐ **C.** The contents of the cyclist's carrier may fall on to the road
- ☐ **D.** The cyclist may wish to turn right at the end of the road

283 When approaching this hazard why should you slow down?

Mark two answers

- [ ] **A.** Because of the bend
- [ ] **B.** Because it's hard to see to the right
- [ ] **C.** Because of approaching traffic
- [ ] **D.** Because of animals crossing
- [ ] **E.** Because of the level crossing

284 A driver's behaviour has upset you. It may help if you

Mark one answer

- [ ] **A.** stop and take a break
- [ ] **B.** shout abusive language
- [ ] **C.** gesture to them with your hand
- [ ] **D.** follow their car, flashing your headlights

285 You are on a dual carriageway. Ahead you see a vehicle with an amber flashing light. What will this be?

Mark one answer

- [ ] **A.** An ambulance
- [ ] **B.** A fire engine
- [ ] **C.** A doctor on call
- [ ] **D.** A disabled person's vehicle

286 You are approaching crossroads. The traffic lights have failed. What should you do?

Mark one answer

- [ ] **A.** Brake and stop only for large vehicles
- [ ] **B.** Brake sharply to a stop before looking
- [ ] **C.** Be prepared to brake sharply to a stop
- [ ] **D.** Be prepared to stop for any traffic

287 Why are place names painted on the road surface?

Mark one answer

- [ ] **A.** To restrict the flow of traffic
- [ ] **B.** To warn you of oncoming traffic
- [ ] **C.** To enable you to change lanes early
- [ ] **D.** To prevent you changing lanes

288 What should the driver of the red car (arrowed) do?

Mark one answer

- [ ] **A.** Wave the pedestrians who are waiting to cross
- [ ] **B.** Wait for the pedestrian in the road to cross
- [ ] **C.** Quickly drive behind the pedestrian in the road
- [ ] **D.** Tell the pedestrian in the road she should not have crossed

289
You are following a slower-moving vehicle on a narrow country road. There is a junction just ahead on the right. What should you do?

Mark one answer

- ☐ **A.** Overtake after checking your mirrors and signalling
- ☐ **B.** Stay behind until you are past the junction
- ☐ **C.** Accelerate quickly to pass before the junction
- ☐ **D.** Slow down and prepare to overtake on the left

290
What should you do as you approach this overhead bridge?

Mark one answer

- ☐ **A.** Move out to the centre of the road before going through
- ☐ **B.** Find another route, this is only for high vehicles
- ☐ **C.** Be prepared to give way to large vehicles in the middle of the road
- ☐ **D.** Move across to the right-hand side before going through

291
Why are mirrors often slightly curved (convex)?

Mark one answer

- ☐ **A.** They give a wider field of vision
- ☐ **B.** They totally cover blind spots
- ☐ **C.** They make it easier to judge the speed of following traffic
- ☐ **D.** They make following traffic look bigger

292
What does the solid white line at the side of the road indicate?

Mark one answer

- ☐ **A.** Traffic lights ahead
- ☐ **B.** Edge of the carriageway
- ☐ **C.** Footpath on the left
- ☐ **D.** Cycle path

293
You are driving towards this level crossing. What would be the first warning of an approaching train?

Mark one answer

- ☐ **A.** Both half barriers down
- ☐ **B.** A steady amber light
- ☐ **C.** One half barrier down
- ☐ **D.** Twin flashing red lights

294 You are driving along this motorway. It is raining. When following this lorry you should

Mark two answers

- [ ] **A.** allow at least a two-second gap
- [ ] **B.** move left and drive on the hard shoulder
- [ ] **C.** allow at least a four-second gap
- [ ] **D.** be aware of spray reducing your vision
- [ ] **E.** move right and stay in the right-hand lane

295 You are behind this cyclist. When the traffic lights change, what should you do?

Mark one answer

- [ ] **A.** Try to move off before the cyclist
- [ ] **B.** Allow the cyclist time and room
- [ ] **C.** Turn right but give the cyclist room
- [ ] **D.** Tap your horn and drive through first

296 You are driving towards this left-hand bend. What dangers should you be aware of?

Mark one answer

- [ ] **A.** A vehicle overtaking you
- [ ] **B.** No white lines in the centre of the road
- [ ] **C.** No sign to warn you of the bend
- [ ] **D.** Pedestrians walking towards you

297 While driving, you see this sign ahead. You should

Mark one answer

- [ ] **A.** stop at the sign
- [ ] **B.** slow, but continue around the bend
- [ ] **C.** slow to a crawl and continue
- [ ] **D.** stop and look for open farm gates

298 Why should the junction on the left be kept clear?

Mark one answer

- ☐ **A.** To allow vehicles to enter and emerge
- ☐ **B.** To allow the bus to reverse
- ☐ **C.** To allow vehicles to make a U-turn
- ☐ **D.** To allow vehicles to park

299 When the traffic lights change to green the white car should

Mark one answer

- ☐ **A.** wait for the cyclist to pull away
- ☐ **B.** move off quickly and turn in front of the cyclist
- ☐ **C.** move close up to the cyclist to beat the lights
- ☐ **D.** sound the horn to warn the cyclist

300 You intend to turn left at the traffic lights. Just before turning you should

Mark one answer

- ☐ **A.** check your right mirror
- ☐ **B.** move close up to the white car
- ☐ **C.** straddle the lanes
- ☐ **D.** check for bicycles on your left

301 You should reduce your speed when driving along this road because

Mark one answer

- ☐ **A.** there is a staggered junction ahead
- ☐ **B.** there is a low bridge ahead
- ☐ **C.** there is a change in the road surface
- ☐ **D.** the road ahead narrows

302 You are driving at 60mph. As you approach this hazard you should

Mark one answer

- ☐ **A.** maintain your speed
- ☐ **B.** reduce your speed
- ☐ **C.** take the next right turn
- ☐ **D.** take the next left turn

303 The traffic ahead of you in the left-hand lane is slowing. You should

Mark two answers

- ☐ **A.** be wary of cars on your right cutting in
- ☐ **B.** accelerate past the vehicles in the left-hand lane
- ☐ **C.** pull up on the left-hand verge
- ☐ **D.** move across and continue in the right-hand lane
- ☐ **E.** slow down, keeping a safe separation distance

304 What might you expect to happen in this situation?

Mark one answer

- ☐ **A.** Traffic will move into the right-hand lane
- ☐ **B.** Traffic speed will increase
- ☐ **C.** Traffic will move into the left-hand lane
- ☐ **D.** Traffic will not need to change position

305 You are driving on a road with several lanes. You see these signs above the lanes. What do they mean?

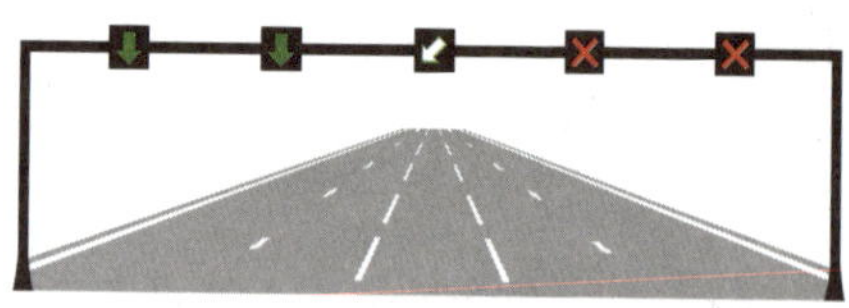

Mark one answer

- ☐ **A.** The two right lanes are open
- ☐ **B.** The two left lanes are open
- ☐ **C.** Traffic in the left lanes should stop
- ☐ **D.** Traffic in the right lanes should stop

306 As a provisional licence holder, you must not drive a motor car

Mark two answers

- ☐ **A.** at more than 40mph
- ☐ **B.** on your own
- ☐ **C.** on the motorway
- ☐ **D.** under the age of 18 years at night
- ☐ **E.** with passengers in the rear seats

307 After passing your driving test, you suffer from ill health. This affects your driving. You MUST

Mark one answer

- ☐ **A.** inform your local police station
- ☐ **B.** avoid using motorways
- ☐ **C.** always drive accompanied
- ☐ **D.** inform the licensing authority

308 You are invited to a pub lunch. You know that you will have to drive in the evening. What is your best course of action?

Mark one answer

- ☐ **A.** Avoid mixing your alcoholic drinks
- ☐ **B.** Not drink any alcohol at all
- ☐ **C.** Have some milk before drinking alcohol
- ☐ **D.** Eat a hot meal with your alcoholic drinks

309 You have been convicted of driving whilst unfit through drink or drugs. You will find this is likely to cause the cost of one of the following to rise considerably. Which one?

Mark one answer

- ☐ **A.** Road fund licence
- ☐ **B.** Insurance premiums
- ☐ **C.** Vehicle test certificate
- ☐ **D.** Driving licence

310 What advice should you give to a driver who has had a few alcoholic drinks at a party?

Mark one answer

- ☐ **A.** Have a strong cup of coffee and then drive home
- ☐ **B.** Drive home carefully and slowly
- ☐ **C.** Go home by public transport
- ☐ **D.** Wait a short while and then drive home

311 You have been taking medicine for a few days which made you feel drowsy. Today you feel better but still need to take the medicine. You should only drive

Mark one answer

- ☐ **A.** if your journey is necessary
- ☐ **B.** at night on quiet roads
- ☐ **C.** if someone goes with you
- ☐ **D.** after checking with your doctor

312 You are about to return home from holiday when you become ill. A doctor prescribes drugs which are likely to affect your driving. You should

Mark one answer

- ☐ **A.** drive only if someone is with you
- ☐ **B.** avoid driving on motorways
- ☐ **C.** not drive yourself
- ☐ **D.** never drive at more than 30mph

313 During periods of illness your ability to drive may be impaired. You MUST

Mark two answers

- ☐ **A.** see your doctor each time before you drive
- ☐ **B.** only take smaller doses of any medicines
- ☐ **C.** be medically fit to drive
- ☐ **D.** not drive after taking certain medicines
- ☐ **E.** take all your medicines with you when you drive

314 You feel drowsy when driving. You should

Mark two answers

- ☐ **A.** stop and rest as soon as possible
- ☐ **B.** turn the heater up to keep you warm and comfortable
- ☐ **C.** make sure you have a good supply of fresh air
- ☐ **D.** continue with your journey but drive more slowly
- ☐ **E.** close the car windows to help you concentrate

315 You are driving along a motorway and become tired. You should

Mark two answers

- ☐ **A.** stop at the next service area and rest
- ☐ **B.** leave the motorway at the next exit and rest
- ☐ **C.** increase your speed and turn up the radio volume
- ☐ **D.** close all your windows and set heating to warm
- ☐ **E.** pull up on the hard shoulder and change drivers

316 You are taking drugs that are likely to affect your driving. What should you do?

Mark one answer

- ☐ **A.** Seek medical advice before driving
- ☐ **B.** Limit your driving to essential journeys
- ☐ **C.** Only drive if accompanied by a full licence-holder
- ☐ **D.** Drive only for short distances

317 You are about to drive home. You feel very tired and have a severe headache. You should

Mark one answer

- ☐ **A.** wait until you are fit and well before driving
- ☐ **B.** drive home, but take a tablet for headaches
- ☐ **C.** drive home if you can stay awake for the journey
- ☐ **D.** wait for a short time, then drive home slowly

318 If you are feeling tired it is best to stop as soon as you can. Until then you should

Mark one answer

- [ ] **A.** increase your speed to find a stopping place quickly
- [ ] **B.** ensure a supply of fresh air
- [ ] **C.** gently tap the steering wheel
- [ ] **D.** keep changing speed to improve concentration

319 If your motorway journey seems boring and you feel drowsy while driving, you should

Mark one answer

- [ ] **A.** open a window and drive to the next service area
- [ ] **B.** stop on the hard shoulder for a sleep
- [ ] **C.** speed up to arrive at your destination sooner
- [ ] **D.** slow down and let other drivers overtake

320 Driving long distances can be tiring. You can prevent this by

Mark three answers

- [ ] **A.** stopping every so often for a walk
- [ ] **B.** opening a window for some fresh air
- [ ] **C.** ensuring plenty of refreshment breaks
- [ ] **D.** completing the journey without stopping
- [ ] **E.** eating a large meal before driving

321 You go to a social event and need to drive a short time after. What precaution should you take?

Mark one answer

- [ ] **A.** Avoid drinking alcohol on an empty stomach
- [ ] **B.** Drink plenty of coffee after drinking alcohol
- [ ] **C.** Avoid drinking alcohol completely
- [ ] **D.** Drink plenty of milk before drinking alcohol

322 You take some cough medicine given to you by a friend. What should you do before driving?

Mark one answer

- [ ] **A.** Ask your friend if taking the medicine affected their driving
- [ ] **B.** Drink some strong coffee one hour before driving
- [ ] **C.** Check the label to see if the medicine will affect your driving
- [ ] **D.** Drive a short distance to see if the medicine is affecting your driving

323 You take the wrong route and find you are on a one-way street. You should

Mark one answer

- [ ] **A.** reverse out of the road
- [ ] **B.** turn round in a side road
- [ ] **C.** continue to the end of the road
- [ ] **D.** reverse into a driveway

324 Which THREE are likely to make you lose concentration while driving?

Mark three answers

- ☐ **A.** Looking at road maps
- ☐ **B.** Listening to loud music
- ☐ **C.** Using your windscreen washers
- ☐ **D.** Looking in your wing mirror
- ☐ **E.** Using a mobile phone

325 You are driving along this road. The driver on the left is reversing from a driveway. You should

Mark one answer

- ☐ **A.** move to the opposite side of the road
- ☐ **B.** drive through as you have priority
- ☐ **C.** sound your horn and be prepared to stop
- ☐ **D.** speed up and drive through quickly

326 You have been involved in an argument before starting your journey. This has made you feel angry. You should

Mark one answer

- ☐ **A.** start to drive, but open a window
- ☐ **B.** drive slower than normal and turn your radio on
- ☐ **C.** have an alcoholic drink to help you relax before driving
- ☐ **D.** calm down before you start to drive

327 You start to feel tired while driving. What should you do?

Mark one answer

- ☐ **A.** Increase your speed slightly
- ☐ **B.** Decrease your speed slightly
- ☐ **C.** Find a less busy route
- ☐ **D.** Pull over at a safe place to rest

328 You are driving on this dual carriageway. Why may you need to slow down?

Mark one answer

- ☐ **A.** There is a broken white line in the centre
- ☐ **B.** There are solid white lines either side
- ☐ **C.** There are road works ahead of you
- ☐ **D.** There are no footpaths

329 You have just been overtaken by this motorcyclist who is cutting in sharply. You should

Mark one answer

- [ ] **A.** sound the horn
- [ ] **B.** brake firmly
- [ ] **C.** keep a safe gap
- [ ] **D.** flash your lights

330 You are about to drive home. You cannot find the glasses you need to wear. You should

Mark one answer

- [ ] **A.** drive home slowly, keeping to quiet roads
- [ ] **B.** borrow a friend's glasses and use those
- [ ] **C.** drive home at night, so that the lights will help you
- [ ] **D.** find a way of getting home without driving

331 Which THREE result from drinking alcohol?

Mark three answers

- [ ] **A.** Less control
- [ ] **B.** A false sense of confidence
- [ ] **C.** Faster reactions
- [ ] **D.** Poor judgement of speed
- [ ] **E.** Greater awareness of danger

332 Which THREE of these are likely effects of drinking alcohol?

Mark three answers

- [ ] **A.** Reduced co-ordination
- [ ] **B.** Increased confidence
- [ ] **C.** Poor judgement
- [ ] **D.** Increased concentration
- [ ] **E.** Faster reactions
- [ ] **F.** Colour blindness

333 How does alcohol affect you?

Mark one answer

- [ ] **A.** It speeds up your reactions
- [ ] **B.** It increases your awareness
- [ ] **C.** It improves your co-ordination
- [ ] **D.** It reduces your concentration

334 Your doctor has given you a course of medicine. Why should you ask how it will affect you?

Mark one answer

- [ ] **A.** Drugs make you a better driver by quickening your reactions
- [ ] **B.** You will have to let your insurance company know about the medicine
- [ ] **C.** Some types of medicine can cause your reactions to slow down
- [ ] **D.** The medicine you take may affect your hearing

335 **You are not sure if your cough medicine will affect you. What TWO things should you do?**

Mark two answers

- [ ] **A.** Ask your doctor
- [ ] **B.** Check the medicine label
- [ ] **C.** Drive if you feel alright
- [ ] **D.** Ask a friend or relative for advice

336 **You are on a motorway. You feel tired. You should**

Mark one answer

- [ ] **A.** carry on but go slowly
- [ ] **B.** leave the motorway at the next exit
- [ ] **C.** complete your journey as quickly as possible
- [ ] **D.** stop on the hard shoulder

337 **You find that you need glasses to read vehicle number plates at the required distance. When MUST you wear them?**

Mark one answer

- [ ] **A.** Only in bad weather conditions
- [ ] **B.** At all times when driving
- [ ] **C.** Only when you think it necessary
- [ ] **D.** Only in bad light or at night time

338 **Which TWO things would help to keep you alert during a long journey?**

Mark two answers

- [ ] **A.** Finishing your journey as fast as you can
- [ ] **B.** Keeping off the motorways and using country roads
- [ ] **C.** Making sure that you get plenty of fresh air
- [ ] **D.** Making regular stops for refreshments

339 **Which of the following types of glasses should NOT be worn when driving at night?**

Mark one answer

- [ ] **A.** Half-moon
- [ ] **B.** Round
- [ ] **C.** Bi-focal
- [ ] **D.** Tinted

340 **Drinking any amount of alcohol is likely to**

Mark three answers

- [ ] **A.** slow down your reactions to hazards
- [ ] **B.** increase the speed of your reactions
- [ ] **C.** worsen your judgement of speed
- [ ] **D.** improve your awareness of danger
- [ ] **E.** give a false sense of confidence

341 **What else can seriously affect your concentration, other than alcoholic drinks?**

Mark three answers

- [ ] **A.** Drugs
- [ ] **B.** Tiredness
- [ ] **C.** Tinted windows
- [ ] **D.** Contact lenses
- [ ] **E.** Loud music

342 **As a driver you find that your eyesight has become very poor. Your optician says they cannot help you. The law says that you should tell**

Mark one answer

- [ ] **A.** the licensing authority
- [ ] **B.** your own doctor
- [ ] **C.** the local police station
- [ ] **D.** another optician

343 For which of these may you use hazard warning lights?

Mark one answer

- [ ] **A.** When driving on a motorway to warn traffic behind of a hazard ahead
- [ ] **B.** When you are double parked on a two-way road
- [ ] **C.** When your direction indicators are not working
- [ ] **D.** When warning oncoming traffic that you intend to stop

344 When should you use hazard warning lights?

Mark one answer

- [ ] **A.** When you are double parked on a two-way road
- [ ] **B.** When your direction indicators are not working
- [ ] **C.** When warning oncoming traffic that you intend to stop
- [ ] **D.** When your vehicle has broken down and is causing an obstruction

345 You want to turn left at this junction. The view of the main road is restricted. What should you do?

Mark one answer

- [ ] **A.** Stay well back and wait to see if something comes
- [ ] **B.** Build up your speed so that you can emerge quickly
- [ ] **C.** Stop and apply the handbrake even if the road is clear
- [ ] **D.** Approach slowly and edge out until you can see more clearly

346 You are driving on a motorway. The traffic ahead is braking sharply because of an accident. How could you warn traffic behind you?

Mark one answer

- [ ] **A.** Briefly use the hazard warning lights
- [ ] **B.** Switch on the hazard warning lights continuously
- [ ] **C.** Briefly use the rear fog lights
- [ ] **D.** Switch on the headlights continuously

347 **When may you use hazard warning lights?**

Mark one answer

- ☐ **A.** To park alongside another car
- ☐ **B.** To park on double yellow lines
- ☐ **C.** When you are being towed
- ☐ **D.** When you have broken down

348 **Hazard warning lights should be used when vehicles are**

Mark one answer

- ☐ **A.** broken down and causing an obstruction
- ☐ **B.** faulty and moving slowly
- ☐ **C.** being towed along a road
- ☐ **D.** reversing into a side road

349 **Some two-way roads are divided into three lanes. Why are these particularly dangerous?**

Mark one answer

- ☐ **A.** Traffic in both directions can use the middle lane to overtake
- ☐ **B.** Traffic can travel faster in poor weather conditions
- ☐ **C.** Traffic can overtake on the left
- ☐ **D.** Traffic uses the middle lane for emergencies only

350 **To avoid an accident when entering a contraflow system, you should**

Mark three answers

- ☐ **A.** reduce speed in good time
- ☐ **B.** switch lanes any time to make progress
- ☐ **C.** choose an appropriate lane early
- ☐ **D.** keep the correct separation distance
- ☐ **E.** increase speed to pass through quickly
- ☐ **F.** follow other motorists closely to avoid long queues

351 **When driving a car fitted with automatic transmission what would you use 'kick down' for?**

Mark one answer

- ☐ **A.** Cruise control
- ☐ **B.** Quick acceleration
- ☐ **C.** Slow braking
- ☐ **D.** Fuel economy

352 **You are waiting to emerge at a junction. Your view is restricted by parked vehicles. What can help you to see traffic on the road you are joining?**

Mark one answer

- ☐ **A.** Looking for traffic behind you
- ☐ **B.** Reflections of traffic in shop windows
- ☐ **C.** Making eye contact with other road users
- ☐ **D.** Checking for traffic in your interior mirror

353 Which sign means that there may be people walking along the road?

Mark one answer

- [ ] **A.**

- [ ] **B.**

- [ ] **C.**

- [ ] **D.**

354 You are turning left at a junction. Pedestrians have started to cross the road. You should

Mark one answer

- [ ] **A.** go on, giving them plenty of room
- [ ] **B.** stop and wave at them to cross
- [ ] **C.** blow your horn and proceed
- [ ] **D.** give way to them

355 You are turning left from a main road into a side road. People are already crossing the road into which you are turning. You should

Mark one answer

- [ ] **A.** continue, as it is your right of way
- [ ] **B.** signal to them to continue crossing
- [ ] **C.** wait and allow them to cross
- [ ] **D.** sound your horn to warn them of your presence

356 You are at a road junction, turning into a minor road. There are pedestrians crossing the minor road. You should

Mark one answer

- [ ] **A.** stop and wave the pedestrians across
- [ ] **B.** sound your horn to let the pedestrians know that you are there
- [ ] **C.** give way to the pedestrians who are already crossing
- [ ] **D.** carry on; the pedestrians should give way to you

357 You are turning left into a side road. What hazards should you be especially aware of?

Mark one answer

- [ ] A. One-way street
- [ ] B. Pedestrians
- [ ] C. Traffic congestion
- [ ] D. Parked vehicles

358 You intend to turn right into a side road. Just before turning you should check for motorcyclists who might be

Mark one answer

- [ ] A. overtaking on your left
- [ ] B. following you closely
- [ ] C. emerging from the side road
- [ ] D. overtaking on your right

359 A toucan crossing is different from other crossings because

Mark one answer

- [ ] A. moped riders can use it
- [ ] B. it is controlled by a traffic warden
- [ ] C. it is controlled by two flashing lights
- [ ] D. cyclists can use it

360 At toucan crossings

Mark two answers

- [ ] A. there is no flashing amber light
- [ ] B. cyclists are not permitted
- [ ] C. there is a continuously flashing amber beacon
- [ ] D. pedestrians and cyclists may cross
- [ ] E. you only stop if someone is waiting to cross

361 What does this sign tell you?

Mark one answer

- [ ] A. No cycling
- [ ] B. Cycle route ahead
- [ ] C. Cycle parking only
- [ ] D. End of cycle route

362 How will a school crossing patrol signal you to stop?

Mark one answer

- [ ] A. By pointing to children on the opposite pavement
- [ ] B. By displaying a red light
- [ ] C. By displaying a stop sign
- [ ] D. By giving you an arm signal

363 Where would you see this sign?

Mark one answer

- [ ] A. In the window of a car taking children to school
- [ ] B. At the side of the road
- [ ] C. At playground areas
- [ ] D. On the rear of a school bus or coach

364 Which sign tells you that pedestrians may be walking in the road as there is no pavement?

Mark one answer

- [ ] **A.**

- [ ] **B.**

- [ ] **C.**

- [ ] **D.**

365 What does this sign mean?

Mark one answer

- [ ] **A.** No route for pedestrians and cyclists
- [ ] **B.** A route for pedestrians only
- [ ] **C.** A route for cyclists only
- [ ] **D.** A route for pedestrians and cyclists

366 You see a pedestrian with a white stick and red band. This means that the person is

Mark one answer

- [ ] **A.** physically disabled
- [ ] **B.** deaf only
- [ ] **C.** blind only
- [ ] **D.** deaf and blind

367 What action would you take when elderly people are crossing the road?

Mark one answer

- [ ] **A.** Wave them across so they know that you have seen them
- [ ] **B.** Be patient and allow them to cross in their own time
- [ ] **C.** Rev the engine to let them know that you are waiting
- [ ] **D.** Tap the horn in case they are hard of hearing

368 You see two elderly pedestrians about to cross the road ahead. You should

Mark one answer

- [ ] **A.** expect them to wait for you to pass
- [ ] **B.** speed up to get past them quickly
- [ ] **C.** stop and wave them across the road
- [ ] **D.** be careful, they may misjudge your speed

369 What does this sign mean?

Mark one answer

- [ ] **A.** Contraflow pedal cycle lane
- [ ] **B.** With-flow pedal cycle lane
- [ ] **C.** Pedal cycles and buses only
- [ ] **D.** No pedal cycles or buses

370 **You are coming up to a roundabout. A cyclist is signalling to turn right. What should you do?**

Mark one answer

- [ ] **A.** Overtake on the right
- [ ] **B.** Give a horn warning
- [ ] **C.** Signal the cyclist to move across
- [ ] **D.** Give the cyclist plenty of room

371 **You are approaching this roundabout and see the cyclist signal right. Why is the cyclist keeping to the left?**

Mark one answer

- [ ] **A.** It is a quicker route for the cyclist
- [ ] **B.** The cyclist is going to turn left instead
- [ ] **C.** The cyclist thinks *The Highway Code* does not apply to bicycles
- [ ] **D.** The cyclist is slower and more vulnerable

372 **When you are overtaking a cyclist you should leave as much room as you would give to a car. What is the main reason for this?**

Mark one answer

- [ ] **A.** The cyclist might change lanes
- [ ] **B.** The cyclist might get off the bike
- [ ] **C.** The cyclist might swerve
- [ ] **D.** The cyclist might have to make a right turn

373 **Which TWO should you allow extra room when overtaking?**

Mark two answers

- [ ] **A.** Motorcycles
- [ ] **B.** Tractors
- [ ] **C.** Bicycles
- [ ] **D.** Road-sweeping vehicles

374 **Why should you look particularly for motorcyclists and cyclists at junctions?**

Mark one answer

- [ ] **A.** They may want to turn into the side road
- [ ] **B.** They may slow down to let you turn
- [ ] **C.** They are harder to see
- [ ] **D.** They might not see you turn

375 **You are waiting to come out of a side road. Why should you watch carefully for motorcycles?**

Mark one answer

- [ ] **A.** Motorcycles are usually faster than cars
- [ ] **B.** Police patrols often use motorcycles
- [ ] **C.** Motorcycles are small and hard to see
- [ ] **D.** Motorcycles have right of way

376 **In daylight, an approaching motorcyclist is using a dipped headlight. Why?**

Mark one answer

- [ ] **A.** So that the rider can be seen more easily
- [ ] **B.** To stop the battery overcharging
- [ ] **C.** To improve the rider's vision
- [ ] **D.** The rider is inviting you to proceed

377 Motorcyclists should wear bright clothing mainly because

Mark one answer

- [ ] **A.** they must do so by law
- [ ] **B.** it helps keep them cool in summer
- [ ] **C.** the colours are popular
- [ ] **D.** drivers often do not see them

378 There is a slow-moving motorcyclist ahead of you. You are unsure what the rider is going to do. You should

Mark one answer

- [ ] **A.** pass on the left
- [ ] **B.** pass on the right
- [ ] **C.** stay behind
- [ ] **D.** move closer

379 Motorcyclists will often look round over their right shoulder just before turning right. This is because

Mark one answer

- [ ] **A.** they need to listen for following traffic
- [ ] **B.** motorcycles do not have mirrors
- [ ] **C.** looking around helps them balance as they turn
- [ ] **D.** they need to check for traffic in their blind area

380 At road junctions which of the following are most vulnerable?

Mark three answers

- [ ] **A.** Cyclists
- [ ] **B.** Motorcyclists
- [ ] **C.** Pedestrians
- [ ] **D.** Car drivers
- [ ] **E.** Lorry drivers

381 Motorcyclists are particularly vulnerable

Mark one answer

- [ ] **A.** when moving off
- [ ] **B.** on dual carriageways
- [ ] **C.** when approaching junctions
- [ ] **D.** on motorways

382 An injured motorcyclist is lying unconscious in the road. You should

Mark one answer

- [ ] **A.** remove the safety helmet
- [ ] **B.** seek medical assistance
- [ ] **C.** move the person off the road
- [ ] **D.** remove the leather jacket

383 You notice horse riders in front. What should you do FIRST?

Mark one answer

- [ ] **A.** Pull out to the middle of the road
- [ ] **B.** Slow down and be ready to stop
- [ ] **C.** Accelerate around them
- [ ] **D.** Signal right

384 **You are approaching a roundabout. There are horses just ahead of you. You should**

Mark two answers
- ☐ **A.** be prepared to stop
- ☐ **B.** treat them like any other vehicle
- ☐ **C.** give them plenty of room
- ☐ **D.** accelerate past as quickly as possible
- ☐ **E.** sound your horn as a warning

385 **Which THREE should you do when passing sheep on a road?**

Mark three answers
- ☐ **A.** Allow plenty of room
- ☐ **B.** Go very slowly
- ☐ **C.** Pass quickly but quietly
- ☐ **D.** Be ready to stop
- ☐ **E.** Briefly sound your horn

386 **At night you see a pedestrian wearing reflective clothing and carrying a bright red light. What does this mean?**

Mark one answer
- ☐ **A.** You are approaching road works
- ☐ **B.** You are approaching an organised walk
- ☐ **C.** You are approaching a slow-moving vehicle
- ☐ **D.** You are approaching an accident black spot

387 **As you approach a pelican crossing the lights change to green. Elderly people are half-way across. You should**

Mark one answer
- ☐ **A.** wave them to cross as quickly as they can
- ☐ **B.** rev your engine to make them hurry
- ☐ **C.** flash your lights in case they have not heard you
- ☐ **D.** wait because they will take longer to cross

388 **There are flashing amber lights under a school warning sign. What action should you take?**

Mark one answer
- ☐ **A.** Reduce speed until you are clear of the area
- ☐ **B.** Keep up your speed and sound the horn
- ☐ **C.** Increase your speed to clear the area quickly
- ☐ **D.** Wait at the lights until they change to green

389 **You are approaching this crossing. You should**

Mark one answer
- [ ] **A.** prepare to slow down and stop
- [ ] **B.** stop and wave the pedestrians across
- [ ] **C.** speed up and pass by quickly
- [ ] **D.** continue unless the pedestrians step out

390 **You see a pedestrian with a dog. The dog has a yellow or burgundy coat. This especially warns you that the pedestrian is**

Mark one answer
- [ ] **A.** elderly
- [ ] **B.** dog training
- [ ] **C.** colour blind
- [ ] **D.** deaf

391 **These road markings must be kept clear to allow**

Mark one answer
- [ ] **A.** schoolchildren to be dropped off
- [ ] **B.** for teachers to park
- [ ] **C.** schoolchildren to be picked up
- [ ] **D.** a clear view of the crossing area

392 **You must not stop on these road markings because you may obstruct**

Mark one answer
- [ ] **A.** children's view of the crossing area
- [ ] **B.** teachers' access to the school
- [ ] **C.** delivery vehicles' access to the school
- [ ] **D.** emergency vehicles' access to the school

393 **The left-hand pavement is closed due to street repairs. What should you do?**

Mark one answer
- [ ] **A.** Watch out for pedestrians walking in the road
- [ ] **B.** Use your right-hand mirror more often
- [ ] **C.** Speed up to get past the road works quicker
- [ ] **D.** Position close to the left-hand kerb

394 **Where would you see this sign?**

Mark one answer
- [ ] **A.** Near a school crossing
- [ ] **B.** At a playground entrance
- [ ] **C.** On a school bus
- [ ] **D.** At a 'pedestrians only' area

395 You are following a motorcyclist on an uneven road. You should

Mark one answer

- A. allow less room so you can be seen in their mirrors
- B. overtake immediately
- C. allow extra room in case they swerve to avoid potholes
- D. allow the same room as normal because road surfaces do not affect motorcyclists

396 You are following two cyclists. They approach a roundabout in the left-hand lane. In which direction should you expect the cyclists to go?

Mark one answer

- A. Left
- B. Right
- C. Any direction
- D. Straight ahead

397 You are travelling behind a moped. You want to turn left just ahead. You should

Mark one answer

- A. overtake the moped before the junction
- B. pull alongside the moped and stay level until just before the junction
- C. sound your horn as a warning and pull in front of the moped
- D. stay behind until the moped has passed the junction

398 Which THREE of the following are hazards motorcyclists present in queues of traffic?

Mark three answers

- A. Cutting in just in front of you
- B. Riding in single file
- C. Passing very close to you
- D. Riding with their headlight on dipped beam
- E. Filtering between the lanes

399 You see a horse rider as you approach a roundabout. They are signalling right but keeping well to the left. You should

Mark one answer

- A. proceed as normal
- B. keep close to them
- C. cut in front of them
- D. stay well back

400 How would you react to drivers who appear to be inexperienced?

Mark one answer

- A. Sound your horn to warn them of your presence
- B. Be patient and prepare for them to react more slowly
- C. Flash your headlights to indicate that it is safe for them to proceed
- D. Overtake them as soon as possible

401 You are following a learner driver who stalls at a junction. You should

Mark one answer

- ☐ **A.** be patient as you expect them to make mistakes
- ☐ **B.** stay very close behind and flash your headlights
- ☐ **C.** start to rev your engine if they take too long to restart
- ☐ **D.** immediately steer around them and drive on

402 You are on a country road. What should you expect to see coming towards you on YOUR side of the road?

Mark one answer

- ☐ **A.** Motorcycles
- ☐ **B.** Bicycles
- ☐ **C.** Pedestrians
- ☐ **D.** Horse riders

403 You are turning left into a side road. Pedestrians are crossing the road near the junction. You must

Mark one answer

- ☐ **A.** wave them on
- ☐ **B.** sound your horn
- ☐ **C.** switch on your hazard lights
- ☐ **D.** wait for them to cross

404 You are following a car driven by an elderly driver. You should

Mark one answer

- ☐ **A.** expect the driver to drive badly
- ☐ **B.** flash your lights and overtake
- ☐ **C.** be aware that the driver's reactions may not be as fast as yours
- ☐ **D.** stay very close behind but be careful

405 You are following a cyclist. You wish to turn left just ahead. You should

Mark one answer

- ☐ **A.** overtake the cyclist before the junction
- ☐ **B.** pull alongside the cyclist and stay level until after the junction
- ☐ **C.** hold back until the cyclist has passed the junction
- ☐ **D.** go around the cyclist on the junction

406 A horse rider is in the left-hand lane approaching a roundabout. You should expect the rider to

Mark one answer

- ☐ **A.** go in any direction
- ☐ **B.** turn right
- ☐ **C.** turn left
- ☐ **D.** go ahead

407 **You have just passed your test. How can you decrease your risk of accidents on the motorway?**

Mark one answer

- [ ] **A.** By keeping up with the car in front
- [ ] **B.** By never going over 40mph
- [ ] **C.** By staying only in the left-hand lane
- [ ] **D.** By taking further training

408 **Powered vehicles used by disabled people are small and hard to see. How do they give early warning when on a dual carriageway?**

Mark one answer

- [ ] **A.** They will have a flashing red light
- [ ] **B.** They will have a flashing green light
- [ ] **C.** They will have a flashing blue light
- [ ] **D.** They will have a flashing amber light

409 **You should never attempt to overtake a cyclist**

Mark one answer

- [ ] **A.** just before you turn left
- [ ] **B.** on a left-hand bend
- [ ] **C.** on a one-way street
- [ ] **D.** on a dual carriageway

410 **Ahead of you there is a moving vehicle with a flashing amber beacon. This means it is**

Mark one answer

- [ ] **A.** slow moving
- [ ] **B.** broken down
- [ ] **C.** a doctor's car
- [ ] **D.** a school crossing patrol

411 **You want to reverse into a side road. You are not sure that the area behind your car is clear. What should you do?**

Mark one answer

- [ ] **A.** Look through the rear window only
- [ ] **B.** Get out and check
- [ ] **C.** Check the mirrors only
- [ ] **D.** Carry on, assuming it is clear

412 **You are about to reverse into a side road. A pedestrian wishes to cross behind you. You should**

Mark one answer

- [ ] **A.** wave to the pedestrian to stop
- [ ] **B.** give way to the pedestrian
- [ ] **C.** wave to the pedestrian to cross
- [ ] **D.** reverse before the pedestrian starts to cross

413 **Who is especially in danger of not being seen as you reverse your car?**

Mark one answer

- [ ] **A.** Motorcyclists
- [ ] **B.** Car drivers
- [ ] **C.** Cyclists
- [ ] **D.** Children

414 **You are reversing around a corner when you notice a pedestrian walking behind you. What should you do?**

Mark one answer

- [ ] **A.** Slow down and wave the pedestrian across
- [ ] **B.** Continue reversing and steer round the pedestrian
- [ ] **C.** Stop and give way
- [ ] **D.** Continue reversing and sound your horn

415 You want to turn right from a junction but your view is restricted by parked vehicles. What should you do?

Mark one answer

- **A.** Move out quickly, but be prepared to stop
- **B.** Sound your horn and pull out if there is no reply
- **C.** Stop, then move slowly forward until you have a clear view
- **D.** Stop, get out and look along the main road to check

416 You are at the front of a queue of traffic waiting to turn right into a side road. Why is it important to check your right mirror just before turning?

Mark one answer

- **A.** To look for pedestrians about to cross
- **B.** To check for overtaking vehicles
- **C.** To make sure the side road is clear
- **D.** To check for emerging traffic

417 What must a driver do at a pelican crossing when the amber light is flashing?

Mark one answer

- **A.** Signal the pedestrian to cross
- **B.** Always wait for the green light before proceeding
- **C.** Give way to any pedestrians on the crossing
- **D.** Wait for the red-and-amber light before proceeding

418 You have stopped at a pelican crossing. A disabled person is crossing slowly in front of you. The lights have now changed to green. You should

Mark two answers

- **A.** allow the person to cross
- **B.** drive in front of the person
- **C.** drive behind the person
- **D.** sound your horn
- **E.** be patient
- **F.** edge forward slowly

419 You are driving past parked cars. You notice a bicycle wheel sticking out between them. What should you do?

Mark one answer

- **A.** Accelerate past quickly and sound your horn
- **B.** Slow down and wave the cyclist across
- **C.** Brake sharply and flash your headlights
- **D.** Slow down and be prepared to stop for a cyclist

420 You are driving past a line of parked cars. You notice a ball bouncing out into the road ahead. What should you do?

Mark one answer

- [ ] **A.** Continue driving at the same speed and sound your horn
- [ ] **B.** Continue driving at the same speed and flash your headlights
- [ ] **C.** Slow down and be prepared to stop for children
- [ ] **D.** Stop and wave the children across to fetch their ball

421 You want to turn right from a main road into a side road. Just before turning you should

Mark one answer

- [ ] **A.** cancel your right-turn signal
- [ ] **B.** select first gear
- [ ] **C.** check for traffic overtaking on your right
- [ ] **D.** stop and set the handbrake

422 You are driving in slow-moving queues of traffic. Just before changing lane you should

Mark one answer

- [ ] **A.** sound the horn
- [ ] **B.** look for motorcyclists filtering through the traffic
- [ ] **C.** give a 'slowing down' arm signal
- [ ] **D.** change down to first gear

423 You are driving in town. There is a bus at the bus stop on the other side of the road. Why should you be careful?

Mark one answer

- [ ] **A.** The bus may have broken down
- [ ] **B.** Pedestrians may come from behind the bus
- [ ] **C.** The bus may move off suddenly
- [ ] **D.** The bus may remain stationary

424 How should you overtake horse riders?

Mark one answer

- [ ] **A.** Drive up close and overtake as soon as possible
- [ ] **B.** Speed is not important but allow plenty of room
- [ ] **C.** Use your horn just once to warn them
- [ ] **D.** Drive slowly and leave plenty of room

425 A friend wants to help you learn to drive. They must be

Mark one answer

- [ ] **A.** over 21 and have held a full licence for at least two years
- [ ] **B.** over 18 and hold an advanced driver's certificate
- [ ] **C.** over 18 and have fully comprehensive insurance
- [ ] **D.** over 21 and have held a full licence for at least three years

426 You are dazzled at night by a vehicle behind you. You should

Mark one answer

- [ ] **A.** set your mirror to anti-dazzle
- [ ] **B.** set your mirror to dazzle the other driver
- [ ] **C.** brake sharply to a stop
- [ ] **D.** switch your rear lights on and off

427 **You have a collision whilst your car is moving. What is the first thing you must do?**

Mark one answer

- [ ] **A.** Stop only if there are injured people
- [ ] **B.** Call the emergency services
- [ ] **C.** Stop at the scene of the accident
- [ ] **D.** Call your insurance company

428 **Yellow zigzag lines on the road outside schools mean**

Mark one answer

- [ ] **A.** sound your horn to alert other road users
- [ ] **B.** stop to allow children to cross
- [ ] **C.** you must not wait or park on these lines
- [ ] **D.** you must not drive over these lines

429 **What do these road markings outside a school mean?**

Mark one answer

- [ ] **A.** You may park here if you are a teacher
- [ ] **B.** Sound your horn before parking
- [ ] **C.** When parking, use your hazard warning lights
- [ ] **D.** You must not wait or park your vehicle here

430 **You are driving on a main road. You intend to turn right into a side road. Just before turning you should**

Mark one answer

- [ ] **A.** adjust your interior mirror
- [ ] **B.** flash your headlamps
- [ ] **C.** steer over to the left
- [ ] **D.** check for traffic overtaking on your right

431 **Why should you allow extra room when overtaking a motorcyclist on a windy day?**

Mark one answer

- [ ] **A.** The rider may turn off suddenly to get out of the wind
- [ ] **B.** The rider may be blown across in front of you
- [ ] **C.** The rider may stop suddenly
- [ ] **D.** The rider may be travelling faster than normal

432 **Which age group of drivers is most likely to be involved in a road accident?**

Mark one answer

- [ ] **A.** 17–25-year-olds
- [ ] **B.** 36–45-year-olds
- [ ] **C.** 46–55-year-olds
- [ ] **D.** over 55-year-olds

433

You are driving towards a zebra crossing. A person in a wheelchair is waiting to cross. What should you do?

Mark one answer

- [ ] **A.** Continue on your way
- [ ] **B.** Wave to the person to cross
- [ ] **C.** Wave to the person to wait
- [ ] **D.** Be prepared to stop

434

Where in particular should you look out for motorcyclists?

Mark one answer

- [ ] **A.** In a filling station
- [ ] **B.** At a road junction
- [ ] **C.** Near a service area
- [ ] **D.** When entering a car park

435

Where should you take particular care to look out for motorcyclists and cyclists?

Mark one answer

- [ ] **A.** On dual carriageways
- [ ] **B.** At junctions
- [ ] **C.** At zebra crossings
- [ ] **D.** On one-way streets

436

The road outside this school is marked with yellow zigzag lines. What do these lines mean?

Mark one answer

- [ ] **A.** You may park on the lines when dropping off schoolchildren
- [ ] **B.** You may park on the lines when picking schoolchildren up
- [ ] **C.** You must not wait or park your vehicle here at all
- [ ] **D.** You must stay with your vehicle if you park here

437 You are about to overtake a slow-moving motorcyclist. Which one of these signs would make you take special care?

Mark one answer

- [ ] **A.** 
- [ ] **B.** 
- [ ] **C.** 
- [ ] **D.** 

438 You are waiting to emerge left from a minor road. A large vehicle is approaching from the right. You have time to turn, but you should wait. Why?

Mark one answer

- [ ] **A.** The large vehicle can easily hide an overtaking vehicle
- [ ] **B.** The large vehicle can turn suddenly
- [ ] **C.** The large vehicle is difficult to steer in a straight line
- [ ] **D.** The large vehicle can easily hide vehicles from the left

439 You are following a long vehicle. It approaches a crossroads and signals left, but moves out to the right. You should

Mark one answer

- [ ] **A.** get closer in order to pass it quickly
- [ ] **B.** stay well back and give it room
- [ ] **C.** assume the signal is wrong and it is really turning right
- [ ] **D.** overtake as it starts to slow down

440 You are following a long vehicle approaching a crossroads. The driver signals right but moves close to the left-hand kerb. What should you do?

Mark one answer

- [ ] **A.** Warn the driver of the wrong signal
- [ ] **B.** Wait behind the long vehicle
- [ ] **C.** Report the driver to the police
- [ ] **D.** Overtake on the right-hand side

441 You are approaching a mini-roundabout. The long vehicle in front is signalling left but positioned over to the right. You should

Mark one answer

- [ ] **A.** sound your horn
- [ ] **B.** overtake on the left
- [ ] **C.** follow the same course as the lorry
- [ ] **D.** keep well back

442 Before overtaking a large vehicle you should keep well back. Why is this?

Mark one answer

- [ ] **A.** To give acceleration space to overtake quickly on blind bends
- [ ] **B.** To get the best view of the road ahead
- [ ] **C.** To leave a gap in case the vehicle stops and rolls back
- [ ] **D.** To offer other drivers a safe gap if they want to overtake you

443 Why is passing a lorry more risky than passing a car?

Mark one answer

- [ ] **A.** Lorries are longer than cars
- [ ] **B.** Lorries may suddenly pull up
- [ ] **C.** The brakes of lorries are not as good
- [ ] **D.** Lorries climb hills more slowly

444 You are travelling behind a bus that pulls up at a bus stop. What should you do?

Mark two answers

- [ ] **A.** Accelerate past the bus sounding your horn
- [ ] **B.** Watch carefully for pedestrians
- [ ] **C.** Be ready to give way to the bus
- [ ] **D.** Pull in closely behind the bus

445 When you approach a bus signalling to move off from a bus stop you should

Mark one answer

- [ ] **A.** get past before it moves
- [ ] **B.** allow it to pull away, if it is safe to do so
- [ ] **C.** flash your headlights as you approach
- [ ] **D.** signal left and wave the bus on

446 Which of these is LEAST likely to be affected by crosswinds?

Mark one answer

- [ ] **A.** Cyclists
- [ ] **B.** Motorcyclists
- [ ] **C.** High-sided vehicles
- [ ] **D.** Cars

447 You are following a large lorry on a wet road. Spray makes it difficult to see. You should

Mark one answer

- [ ] **A.** drop back until you can see better
- [ ] **B.** put your headlights on full beam
- [ ] **C.** keep close to the lorry, away from the spray
- [ ] **D.** speed up and overtake quickly

448 What should you do as you approach this lorry?

Mark one answer

- [ ] **A.** Slow down and be prepared to wait
- [ ] **B.** Make the lorry wait for you
- [ ] **C.** Flash your lights at the lorry
- [ ] **D.** Move to the right-hand side of the road

449 You are following a large articulated vehicle. It is going to turn left into a narrow road. What action should you take?

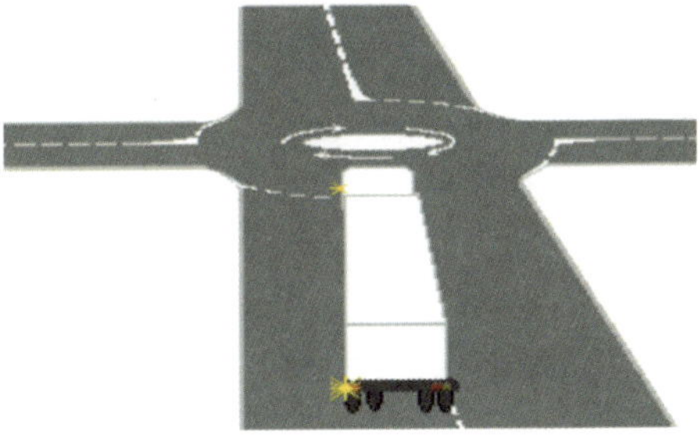

Mark one answer

- [ ] **A.** Move out and overtake on the right
- [ ] **B.** Pass on the left as the vehicle moves out
- [ ] **C.** Be prepared to stop behind
- [ ] **D.** Overtake quickly before the lorry moves out

450 You keep well back while waiting to overtake a large vehicle. A car fills the gap. You should

Mark one answer

- [ ] **A.** sound your horn
- [ ] **B.** drop back further
- [ ] **C.** flash your headlights
- [ ] **D.** start to overtake

451 You are following a large vehicle approaching crossroads. The driver signals to turn left. What should you do?

Mark one answer

- [ ] **A.** Overtake if you can leave plenty of room
- [ ] **B.** Overtake only if there are no oncoming vehicles
- [ ] **C.** Do not overtake until the vehicle begins to turn
- [ ] **D.** Do not overtake when at or approaching a junction

452 You are following a long lorry. The driver signals to turn left into a narrow road. What should you do?

Mark one answer

- ☐ **A.** Overtake on the left before the lorry reaches the junction
- ☐ **B.** Overtake on the right as soon as the lorry slows down
- ☐ **C.** Do not overtake unless you can see there is no oncoming traffic
- ☐ **D.** Do not overtake, stay well back and be prepared to stop

453 You wish to overtake a long, slow-moving vehicle on a busy road. You should

Mark one answer

- ☐ **A.** follow it closely and keep moving out to see the road ahead
- ☐ **B.** flash your headlights for the oncoming traffic to give way
- ☐ **C.** stay behind until the driver waves you past
- ☐ **D.** keep well back until you can see that it is clear

454 It is very windy. You are behind a motorcyclist who is overtaking a high-sided vehicle. What should you do?

Mark one answer

- ☐ **A.** Overtake the motorcyclist immediately
- ☐ **B.** Keep well back
- ☐ **C.** Stay level with the motorcyclist
- ☐ **D.** Keep close to the motorcyclist

455 It is very windy. You are about to overtake a motorcyclist. You should

Mark one answer

- ☐ **A.** overtake slowly
- ☐ **B.** allow extra room
- ☐ **C.** sound your horn
- ☐ **D.** keep close as you pass

456 You are towing a caravan. Which is the safest type of rear-view mirror to use?

Mark one answer

- ☐ **A.** Interior wide-angle mirror
- ☐ **B.** Extended-arm side mirrors
- ☐ **C.** Ordinary door mirrors
- ☐ **D.** Ordinary interior mirror

457 You are driving in town. Ahead of you a bus is at a bus stop. Which TWO of the following should you do?

Mark two answers

- ☐ **A.** Be prepared to give way if the bus suddenly moves off
- ☐ **B.** Continue at the same speed but sound your horn as a warning
- ☐ **C.** Watch carefully for the sudden appearance of pedestrians
- ☐ **D.** Pass the bus as quickly as you possibly can

458 You are driving in heavy traffic on a wet road. Spray makes it difficult to be seen. You should use your

Mark two answers

- [ ] **A.** full beam headlights
- [ ] **B.** rear fog lights if visibility is less than 100 metres (328 feet)
- [ ] **C.** rear fog lights if visibility is more than 100 metres (328 feet)
- [ ] **D.** dipped headlights
- [ ] **E.** sidelights only

459 You are driving along this road. What should you be prepared to do?

Mark one answer

- [ ] **A.** Sound your horn and continue
- [ ] **B.** Slow down and give way
- [ ] **C.** Report the driver to the police
- [ ] **D.** Squeeze through the gap

460 As a driver why should you be more careful where trams operate?

Mark one answer

- [ ] **A.** Because they do not have a horn
- [ ] **B.** Because they do not stop for cars
- [ ] **C.** Because they do not have lights
- [ ] **D.** Because they cannot steer to avoid you

461 It is a very windy day and you are about to overtake a cyclist. What should you do?

Mark one answer

- [ ] **A.** Overtake very closely
- [ ] **B.** Keep close as you pass
- [ ] **C.** Sound your horn repeatedly
- [ ] **D.** Allow extra room

462 Powered vehicles, such as wheelchairs or scooters, used by disabled people have a maximum speed of

Mark one answer

- [ ] **A.** 8mph
- [ ] **B.** 12mph
- [ ] **C.** 16mph
- [ ] **D.** 20mph

463 In front of you is a powered vehicle (powered wheelchair) driven by a disabled person. These vehicles have a maximum speed of

Mark one answer

- [ ] **A.** 8mph
- [ ] **B.** 18mph
- [ ] **C.** 28mph
- [ ] **D.** 38mph

464 In which THREE of these situations may you overtake another vehicle on the left?

Mark three answers

- ☐ **A.** When you are in a one-way street
- ☐ **B.** When approaching a motorway slip road where you will be turning off
- ☐ **C.** When the vehicle in front is signalling to turn right
- ☐ **D.** When a slower vehicle is travelling in the right-hand lane of a dual carriageway
- ☐ **E.** In slow-moving traffic queues when traffic in the right-hand lane is moving more slowly

465 You are travelling in very heavy rain. Your overall stopping distance is likely to be

Mark one answer

- ☐ **A.** doubled
- ☐ **B.** halved
- ☐ **C.** up to ten times greater
- ☐ **D.** no different

466 Which TWO of the following are correct? When overtaking at night you should

Mark two answers

- ☐ **A.** wait until a bend so that you can see the oncoming headlights
- ☐ **B.** sound your horn twice before moving out
- ☐ **C.** be careful because you can see less
- ☐ **D.** beware of bends in the road ahead
- ☐ **E.** put headlights on full beam

467 When may you wait in a box junction?

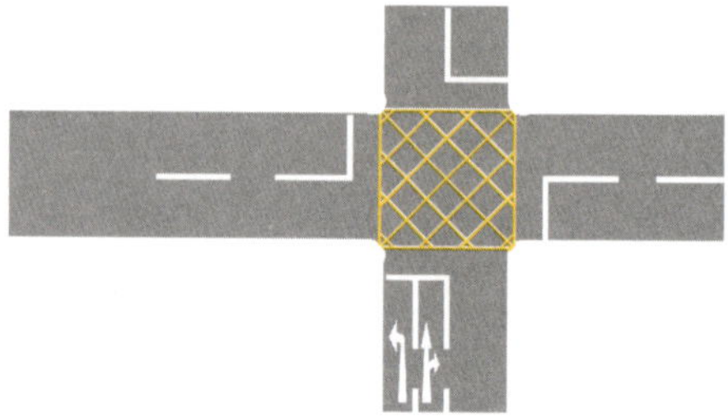

Mark one answer

- ☐ **A.** When you are stationary in a queue of traffic
- ☐ **B.** When approaching a pelican crossing
- ☐ **C.** When approaching a zebra crossing
- ☐ **D.** When oncoming traffic prevents you turning right

468 Which of these plates normally appear with this road sign?

Mark one answer

☐ **A.**

☐ **B.**

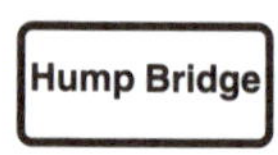

☐ **C.**

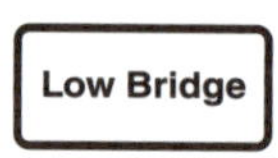

☐ **D.**

469 Areas reserved for trams may have

Mark three answers
- [ ] **A.** metal studs around them
- [ ] **B.** white line markings
- [ ] **C.** zigzag markings
- [ ] **D.** a different coloured surface
- [ ] **E.** yellow hatch markings
- [ ] **F.** a different surface texture

470 Traffic calming measures are used to

Mark one answer
- [ ] **A.** stop road rage
- [ ] **B.** help overtaking
- [ ] **C.** slow traffic down
- [ ] **D.** help parking

471 Why should you always reduce your speed when travelling in fog?

Mark one answer
- [ ] **A.** The brakes do not work as well
- [ ] **B.** You will be dazzled by other headlights
- [ ] **C.** The engine will take longer to warm up
- [ ] **D.** It is more difficult to see events ahead

472 You are on a motorway in fog. The left-hand edge of the motorway can be identified by reflective studs. What colour are they?

Mark one answer
- [ ] **A.** Green
- [ ] **B.** Amber
- [ ] **C.** Red
- [ ] **D.** White

473 A rumble device is designed to

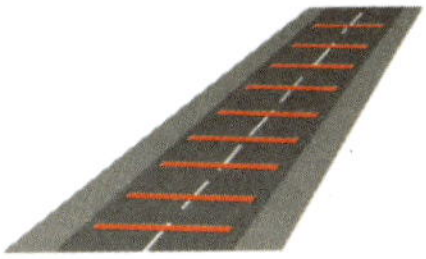

Mark two answers
- [ ] **A.** give directions
- [ ] **B.** prevent cattle escaping
- [ ] **C.** alert you to low tyre pressure
- [ ] **D.** alert you to a hazard
- [ ] **E.** encourage you to reduce speed

474 You are on a narrow road at night. A slower-moving vehicle ahead has been signalling right for some time. What should you do?

Mark one answer
- [ ] **A.** Overtake on the left
- [ ] **B.** Flash your headlights before overtaking
- [ ] **C.** Signal right and sound your horn
- [ ] **D.** Wait for the signal to be cancelled before overtaking

475 After this hazard you should test your brakes. Why is this?

Mark one answer
- [ ] **A.** You will be on a slippery road
- [ ] **B.** Your brakes will be soaking wet
- [ ] **C.** You will be going down a long hill
- [ ] **D.** You will have just crossed a long bridge

476 You have to make a journey in foggy conditions. You should

Mark one answer

- [ ] **A.** follow other vehicles' tail-lights closely
- [ ] **B.** avoid using dipped headlights
- [ ] **C.** leave plenty of time for your journey
- [ ] **D.** keep two seconds behind other vehicles

477 You see a vehicle coming towards you on a single-track road. You should

Mark one answer

- [ ] **A.** go back to the main road
- [ ] **B.** do an emergency stop
- [ ] **C.** stop at a passing place
- [ ] **D.** put on your hazard warning lights

478 You are overtaking a car at night. You must be sure that

Mark one answer

- [ ] **A.** you flash your headlights before overtaking
- [ ] **B.** you select a higher gear
- [ ] **C.** you have switched your lights to full beam before overtaking
- [ ] **D.** you do not dazzle other road users

479 You are on a road which has speed humps. A driver in front is travelling slower than you. You should

Mark one answer

- [ ] **A.** sound your horn
- [ ] **B.** overtake as soon as you can
- [ ] **C.** flash your headlights
- [ ] **D.** slow down and stay behind

480 You are following other vehicles in fog with your lights on. How else can you reduce the chances of being involved in an accident?

Mark one answer

- [ ] **A.** Keep close to the vehicle in front
- [ ] **B.** Use your main beam instead of dipped headlights
- [ ] **C.** Keep together with the faster vehicles
- [ ] **D.** Reduce your speed and increase the gap

481 You see these markings on the road. Why are they there?

Mark one answer

- [ ] **A.** To show a safe distance between vehicles
- [ ] **B.** To keep the area clear of traffic
- [ ] **C.** To make you aware of your speed
- [ ] **D.** To warn you to change direction

482 When MUST you use dipped headlights during the day?

Mark one answer

- [ ] **A.** All the time
- [ ] **B.** Along narrow streets
- [ ] **C.** In poor visibility
- [ ] **D.** When parking

83 What are TWO main reasons why coasting downhill is wrong?

k two answers

- **A.** Fuel consumption will be higher
- **B.** The vehicle will get faster
- **C.** It puts more wear and tear on the tyres
- **D.** You have less braking and steering control
- **E.** It damages the engine

84 Hills can affect the performance of your vehicle. Which TWO apply when driving up steep hills?

k two answers

- **A.** Higher gears will pull better
- **B.** You will slow down sooner
- **C.** Overtaking will be easier
- **D.** The engine will work harder
- **E.** The steering will feel heavier

85 Why is travelling in neutral for long distances (known as coasting) wrong?

rk one answer

- **A.** It will cause the car to skid
- **B.** It will make the engine stall
- **C.** The engine will run faster
- **D.** There is no engine braking

486 You are driving on the motorway in windy conditions. When passing high-sided vehicles you should

ark one answer

- **A.** increase your speed
- **B.** be wary of a sudden gust
- **C.** drive alongside very closely
- **D.** expect normal conditions

487 To correct a rear-wheel skid you should

Mark one answer

- **A.** not steer at all
- **B.** steer away from it
- **C.** steer into it
- **D.** apply your handbrake

488 You have to make a journey in fog. What are the TWO most important things you should do before you set out?

Mark two answers

- **A.** Top up the radiator with antifreeze
- **B.** Make sure that you have a warning triangle in the vehicle
- **C.** Check that your lights are working
- **D.** Check the battery
- **E.** Make sure that the windows are clean

489 You are driving in fog. Why should you keep well back from the vehicle in front?

Mark one answer

- **A.** In case it changes direction suddenly
- **B.** In case its fog lights dazzle you
- **C.** In case it stops suddenly
- **D.** In case its brake lights dazzle you

490 You should switch your rear fog lights on when visibility drops below

Mark one answer

- **A.** your overall stopping distance
- **B.** ten car lengths
- **C.** 200 metres (656 feet)
- **D.** 100 metres (328 feet)

491 Whilst driving, the fog clears and you can see more clearly. You must remember to

Mark one answer

- [ ] **A.** switch off the fog lights
- [ ] **B.** reduce your speed
- [ ] **C.** switch off the demister
- [ ] **D.** close any open windows

492 You have to park on the road in fog. You should

Mark one answer

- [ ] **A.** leave sidelights on
- [ ] **B.** leave dipped headlights and fog lights on
- [ ] **C.** leave dipped headlights on
- [ ] **D.** leave main beam headlights on

493 On a foggy day you unavoidably have to park your car on the road. You should

Mark one answer

- [ ] **A.** leave your headlights on
- [ ] **B.** leave your fog lights on
- [ ] **C.** leave your sidelights on
- [ ] **D.** leave your hazard lights on

494 You are travelling at night. You are dazzled by headlights coming towards you. You should

Mark one answer

- [ ] **A.** pull down your sun visor
- [ ] **B.** slow down or stop
- [ ] **C.** switch on your main beam headlights
- [ ] **D.** put your hand over your eyes

495 Which FOUR of the following may apply when dealing with this hazard?

Mark four answers

- [ ] **A.** It could be more difficult in winter
- [ ] **B.** Use a low gear and drive slowly
- [ ] **C.** Use a high gear to prevent wheelspin
- [ ] **D.** Test your brakes afterwards
- [ ] **E.** Always switch on fog lamps
- [ ] **F.** There may be a depth gauge

496 Front fog lights may be used ONLY if

Mark one answer

- [ ] **A.** visibility is seriously reduced
- [ ] **B.** they are fitted above the bumper
- [ ] **C.** they are not as bright as the headlights
- [ ] **D.** an audible warning device is used

497 Front fog lights may be used ONLY if

Mark one answer

- [ ] **A.** your headlights are not working
- [ ] **B.** they are operated with rear fog lights
- [ ] **C.** they were fitted by the vehicle manufacturer
- [ ] **D.** visibility is seriously reduced

498 You are driving with your front fog lights switched on. Earlier fog has now cleared. What should you do?

Mark one answer

- [ ] **A.** Leave them on if other drivers have their lights on
- [ ] **B.** Switch them off as long as visibility remains good
- [ ] **C.** Flash them to warn oncoming traffic that it is foggy
- [ ] **D.** Drive with them on instead of your headlights

499 Front fog lights should be used ONLY when

Mark one answer

- [ ] **A.** travelling in very light rain
- [ ] **B.** visibility is seriously reduced
- [ ] **C.** daylight is fading
- [ ] **D.** driving after midnight

500 Why is it dangerous to leave rear fog lights on when they are not needed?

Mark two answers

- [ ] **A.** Brake lights are less clear
- [ ] **B.** Following drivers can be dazzled
- [ ] **C.** Electrical systems could be overloaded
- [ ] **D.** Direction indicators may not work properly
- [ ] **E.** The battery could fail

501 You are driving on a clear dry night with your rear fog lights switched on. This may

Mark two answers

- [ ] **A.** reduce glare from the road surface
- [ ] **B.** make other drivers think you are braking
- [ ] **C.** give a better view of the road ahead
- [ ] **D.** dazzle following drivers
- [ ] **E.** help your indicators to be seen more clearly

502 You have just driven out of fog. Visibility is now good. You MUST

Mark one answer

- [ ] **A.** switch off all your fog lights
- [ ] **B.** keep your rear fog lights on
- [ ] **C.** keep your front fog lights on
- [ ] **D.** leave fog lights on in case fog returns

503 You forget to switch off your rear fog lights when the fog has cleared. This may

Mark three answers

- [ ] **A.** dazzle other road users
- [ ] **B.** reduce battery life
- [ ] **C.** cause brake lights to be less clear
- [ ] **D.** be breaking the law
- [ ] **E.** seriously affect engine power

504 You have been driving in thick fog which has now cleared. You must switch OFF your rear fog lights because

Mark one answer

- [ ] **A.** they use a lot of power from the battery
- [ ] **B.** they make your brake lights less clear
- [ ] **C.** they will cause dazzle in your rear-view mirror
- [ ] **D.** they may not be properly adjusted

505 Front fog lights should be used

Mark one answer

- ☐ **A.** when visibility is reduced to 100 metres (328 feet)
- ☐ **B.** as a warning to oncoming traffic
- ☐ **C.** when driving during the hours of darkness
- ☐ **D.** in any conditions and at any time

506 Using rear fog lights in clear daylight will

Mark one answer

- ☐ **A.** be useful when towing a trailer
- ☐ **B.** give extra protection
- ☐ **C.** dazzle other drivers
- ☐ **D.** make following drivers keep back

507 Using front fog lights in clear daylight will

Mark one answer

- ☐ **A.** flatten the battery
- ☐ **B.** dazzle other drivers
- ☐ **C.** improve your visibility
- ☐ **D.** increase your awareness

508 You may use front fog lights with headlights ONLY when visibility is reduced to less than

Mark one answer

- ☐ **A.** 100 metres (328 feet)
- ☐ **B.** 200 metres (656 feet)
- ☐ **C.** 300 metres (984 feet)
- ☐ **D.** 400 metres (1,312 feet)

509 You may drive with front fog lights switched on

Mark one answer

- ☐ **A.** when visibility is less than 100 metres (328 feet)
- ☐ **B.** at any time to be noticed
- ☐ **C.** instead of headlights on high-speed roads
- ☐ **D.** when dazzled by the lights of oncoming vehicles

510 Chains can be fitted to your wheels to help prevent

Mark one answer

- ☐ **A.** damage to the road surface
- ☐ **B.** wear to the tyres
- ☐ **C.** skidding in deep snow
- ☐ **D.** the brakes locking

511 Holding the clutch pedal down or rolling in neutral for too long while driving will

Mark one answer

- ☐ **A.** use more fuel
- ☐ **B.** cause the engine to overheat
- ☐ **C.** reduce your control
- ☐ **D.** improve tyre wear

512 How can you use the engine of your vehicle to control your speed?

Mark one answer

- A. By changing to a lower gear
- B. By selecting reverse gear
- C. By changing to a higher gear
- D. By selecting neutral

513 You are driving down a steep hill. Why could keeping the clutch down or rolling in neutral for too long be dangerous?

Mark one answer

- A. Fuel consumption will be higher
- B. Your vehicle will pick up speed
- C. It will damage the engine
- D. It will wear tyres out more quickly

514 Why could keeping the clutch down or selecting neutral for long periods of time be dangerous?

Mark one answer

- A. Fuel spillage will occur
- B. Engine damage may be caused
- C. You will have less steering and braking control
- D. It will wear tyres out more quickly

515 You are driving on an icy road. What distance should you drive from the car in front?

Mark one answer

- A. four times the normal distance
- B. six times the normal distance
- C. eight times the normal distance
- D. ten times the normal distance

516 You are on a well-lit motorway at night. You must

Mark one answer

- A. use only your sidelights
- B. always use your headlights
- C. always use rear fog lights
- D. use headlights only in bad weather

517 You are on a motorway at night with other vehicles just ahead of you. Which lights should you have on?

Mark one answer

- A. Front fog lights
- B. Main beam headlights
- C. Sidelights only
- D. Dipped headlights

518 Which THREE of the following will affect your stopping distance?

Mark three answers

- A. How fast you are going
- B. The tyres on your vehicle
- C. The time of day
- D. The weather
- E. The street lighting

519 You are on a motorway at night. You MUST have your headlights switched on unless

Mark one answer

- A. there are vehicles close in front of you
- B. you are travelling below 50mph
- C. the motorway is lit
- D. your vehicle is broken down on the hard shoulder

520 You will feel the effects of engine braking when you

Mark one answer
- ☐ **A.** only use the handbrake
- ☐ **B.** only use neutral
- ☐ **C.** change to a lower gear
- ☐ **D.** change to a higher gear

521 Daytime visibility is poor but not seriously reduced. You should switch on

Mark one answer
- ☐ **A.** headlights and fog lights
- ☐ **B.** front fog lights
- ☐ **C.** dipped headlights
- ☐ **D.** rear fog lights

522 Why are vehicles fitted with rear fog lights?

Mark one answer
- ☐ **A.** To be seen when driving at high speed
- ☐ **B.** To use if broken down in a dangerous position
- ☐ **C.** To make them more visible in thick fog
- ☐ **D.** To warn drivers following closely to drop back

523 While you are driving in fog, it becomes necessary to use front fog lights. You should

Mark one answer
- ☐ **A.** only turn them on in heavy traffic conditions
- ☐ **B.** remember not to use them on motorways
- ☐ **C.** only use them on dual carriageways
- ☐ **D.** remember to switch them off as visibility improves

524 When snow is falling heavily you should

Mark one answer
- ☐ **A.** only drive with your hazard lights on
- ☐ **B.** not drive unless you have a mobile phone
- ☐ **C.** only drive when your journey is short
- ☐ **D.** not drive unless it is essential

525 You are driving down a long steep hill. You suddenly notice your brakes are not working as well as normal. What is the usual cause of this?

Mark one answer
- ☐ **A.** The brakes overheating
- ☐ **B.** Air in the brake fluid
- ☐ **C.** Oil on the brakes
- ☐ **D.** Badly adjusted brakes

526 The road is wet. Why might a motorcyclist steer round drain covers on a bend?

Mark one answer
- ☐ **A.** To avoid puncturing the tyres on the edge of the drain covers
- ☐ **B.** To prevent the motorcycle sliding on the metal drain covers
- ☐ **C.** To help judge the bend using the drain covers as marker points
- ☐ **D.** To avoid splashing pedestrians on the pavement

527 Which FOUR of these must NOT use motorways?

Mark four answers

- [ ] **A.** Learner car drivers
- [ ] **B.** Motorcycles over 50cc
- [ ] **C.** Double-deck buses
- [ ] **D.** Farm tractors
- [ ] **E.** Horse riders
- [ ] **F.** Cyclists

528 Which FOUR of these must NOT use motorways?

Mark four answers

- [ ] **A.** Learner car drivers
- [ ] **B.** Motorcycles over 50cc
- [ ] **C.** Double-deck buses
- [ ] **D.** Farm tractors
- [ ] **E.** Learner motorcyclists
- [ ] **F.** Cyclists

529 Immediately after joining a motorway you should normally

Mark one answer

- [ ] **A.** try to overtake
- [ ] **B.** re-adjust your mirrors
- [ ] **C.** position your vehicle in the centre lane
- [ ] **D.** keep in the left-hand lane

530 When joining a motorway you must always

Mark one answer

- [ ] **A.** use the hard shoulder
- [ ] **B.** stop at the end of the acceleration lane
- [ ] **C.** come to a stop before joining the motorway
- [ ] **D.** give way to traffic already on the motorway

531 What is the national speed limit for cars and motorcycles in the centre lane of a three-lane motorway?

Mark one answer

- [ ] **A.** 40mph
- [ ] **B.** 50mph
- [ ] **C.** 60mph
- [ ] **D.** 70mph

532 What is the national speed limit on motorways for cars and motorcycles?

Mark one answer

- [ ] **A.** 30mph
- [ ] **B.** 50mph
- [ ] **C.** 60mph
- [ ] **D.** 70mph

533 The left-hand lane on a three-lane motorway is for use by

Mark one answer

- [ ] **A.** any vehicle
- [ ] **B.** large vehicles only
- [ ] **C.** emergency vehicles only
- [ ] **D.** slow vehicles only

534 What is the right-hand lane used for on a three-lane motorway?

Mark one answer

- [ ] **A.** Emergency vehicles only
- [ ] **B.** Overtaking
- [ ] **C.** Vehicles towing trailers
- [ ] **D.** Coaches only

535 Which of these IS NOT allowed to travel in the right-hand lane of a three-lane motorway?

Mark one answer

- [ ] **A.** A small delivery van
- [ ] **B.** A motorcycle
- [ ] **C.** A vehicle towing a trailer
- [ ] **D.** A motorcycle and sidecar

536 You are travelling on a motorway. You decide you need a rest. You should

Mark two answers

- [ ] **A.** stop on the hard shoulder
- [ ] **B.** go to a service area
- [ ] **C.** park on the slip road
- [ ] **D.** park on the central reservation
- [ ] **E.** leave at the next exit

537 You break down on a motorway. You need to call for help. Why may it be better to use an emergency roadside telephone rather than a mobile phone?

Mark one answer

- [ ] **A.** It connects you to a local garage
- [ ] **B.** Using a mobile phone will distract other drivers
- [ ] **C.** It allows easy location by the emergency services
- [ ] **D.** Mobile phones do not work on motorways

538 What should you use the hard shoulder of a motorway for?

Mark one answer

- [ ] **A.** Stopping in an emergency
- [ ] **B.** Leaving the motorway
- [ ] **C.** Stopping when you are tired
- [ ] **D.** Joining the motorway

539 After a breakdown you need to rejoin the main carriageway of a motorway from the hard shoulder. You should

Mark one answer

- [ ] **A.** move out onto the carriageway then build up your speed
- [ ] **B.** move out onto the carriageway using your hazard lights
- [ ] **C.** gain speed on the hard shoulder before moving out onto the carriageway
- [ ] **D.** wait on the hard shoulder until someone flashes their headlights at you

540 A crawler lane on a motorway is found

Mark one answer

- [ ] **A.** on a steep gradient
- [ ] **B.** before a service area
- [ ] **C.** before a junction
- [ ] **D.** along the hard shoulder

541 You are on a motorway. There are red flashing lights above every lane. You must

Mark one answer

- [ ] **A.** pull on to the hard shoulder
- [ ] **B.** slow down and watch for further signals
- [ ] **C.** leave at the next exit
- [ ] **D.** stop and wait

542 You are in the right-hand lane on a motorway. You see these overhead signs. This means

Mark one answer

- [ ] **A.** move to the left and reduce your speed to 50mph
- [ ] **B.** there are road works 50 metres (55 yards) ahead
- [ ] **C.** use the hard shoulder until you have passed the hazard
- [ ] **D.** leave the motorway at the next exit

543 What do these motorway signs show?

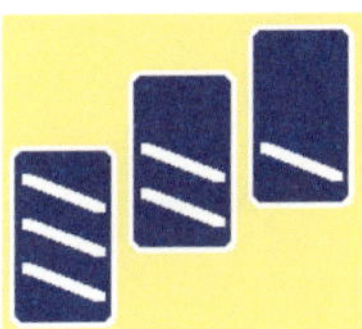

Mark one answer

- [ ] **A.** They are countdown markers to a bridge
- [ ] **B.** They are distance markers to the next telephone
- [ ] **C.** They are countdown markers to the next exit
- [ ] **D.** They warn of a police control ahead

544 On a motorway the amber reflective studs can be found between

Mark one answer

- [ ] **A.** the hard shoulder and the carriageway
- [ ] **B.** the acceleration lane and the carriageway
- [ ] **C.** the central reservation and the carriageway
- [ ] **D.** each pair of the lanes

545 What colour are the reflective studs between the lanes on a motorway?

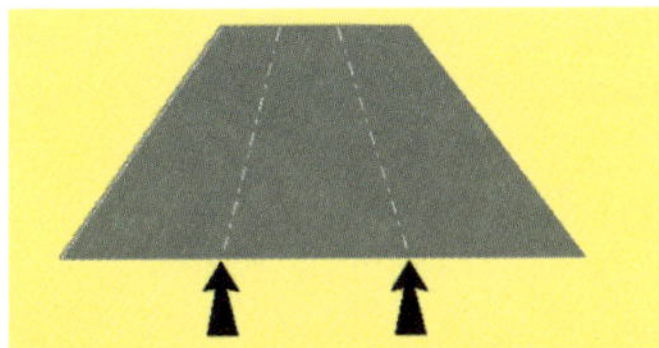

Mark one answer

- [ ] **A.** Green
- [ ] **B.** Amber
- [ ] **C.** White
- [ ] **D.** Red

546 What colour are the reflective studs between a motorway and its slip road?

Mark one answer

- [ ] **A.** Amber
- [ ] **B.** White
- [ ] **C.** Green
- [ ] **D.** Red

547 You are allowed to stop on a motorway when you

Mark one answer

- [ ] **A.** need to walk and get fresh air
- [ ] **B.** wish to pick up hitchhikers
- [ ] **C.** are told to do so by flashing red lights
- [ ] **D.** need to use a mobile telephone

548 You have broken down on a motorway. To find the nearest emergency telephone you should always walk

Mark one answer

- [ ] **A.** with the traffic flow
- [ ] **B.** facing oncoming traffic
- [ ] **C.** in the direction shown on the marker posts
- [ ] **D.** in the direction of the nearest exit

549 You are travelling along the left-hand lane of a three-lane motorway. Traffic is joining from a slip road. You should

Mark one answer

- [ ] **A.** race the other vehicles
- [ ] **B.** move to another lane
- [ ] **C.** maintain a steady speed
- [ ] **D.** switch on your hazard flashers

550 You are joining a motorway. Why is it important to make full use of the slip road?

Mark one answer

- [ ] **A.** Because there is space available to turn round if you need to
- [ ] **B.** To allow you direct access to the overtaking lanes
- [ ] **C.** To build up a speed similar to traffic on the motorway
- [ ] **D.** Because you can continue on the hard shoulder

551 How should you use the emergency telephone on a motorway?

Mark one answer

- [ ] **A.** Stay close to the carriageway
- [ ] **B.** Face the oncoming traffic
- [ ] **C.** Keep your back to the traffic
- [ ] **D.** Stand on the hard shoulder

552 You are on a motorway. What colour are the reflective studs on the left of the carriageway?

Mark one answer

- [ ] **A.** Green
- [ ] **B.** Red
- [ ] **C.** White
- [ ] **D.** Amber

553 On a three-lane motorway which lane should you normally use?

Mark one answer

- [ ] **A.** Left
- [ ] **B.** Right
- [ ] **C.** Centre
- [ ] **D.** Either the right or centre

554 A basic rule when on motorways is

Mark one answer

- [ ] **A.** use the lane that has least traffic
- [ ] **B.** keep to the left-hand lane unless overtaking
- [ ] **C.** overtake on the side that is clearest
- [ ] **D.** try to keep above 50mph to prevent congestion

555 **When going through a contraflow system on a motorway you should**

Mark one answer

- [ ] **A.** ensure that you do not exceed 30mph
- [ ] **B.** keep a good distance from the vehicle ahead
- [ ] **C.** switch lanes to keep the traffic flowing
- [ ] **D.** stay close to the vehicle ahead to reduce queues

556 **You are on a three-lane motorway. There are red reflective studs on your left and white ones to your right. Where are you?**

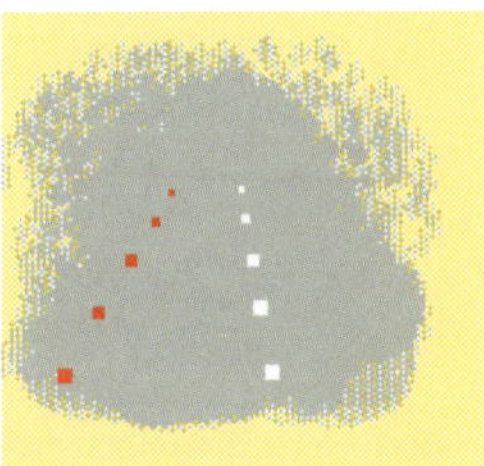

Mark one answer

- [ ] **A.** In the right-hand lane
- [ ] **B.** In the middle lane
- [ ] **C.** On the hard shoulder
- [ ] **D.** In the left-hand lane

557 **When should you stop on a motorway?**

Mark three answers

- [ ] **A.** If you have to read a map
- [ ] **B.** When you are tired and need a rest
- [ ] **C.** If red lights show above every lane
- [ ] **D.** When told to by the police
- [ ] **E.** If your mobile phone rings
- [ ] **F.** In an emergency or a breakdown

558 **You are approaching road works on a motorway. What should you do?**

Mark one answer

- [ ] **A.** Speed up to clear the area quickly
- [ ] **B.** Always use the hard shoulder
- [ ] **C.** Obey all speed limits
- [ ] **D.** Stay very close to the vehicle in front

559 **On motorways you should never overtake on the left unless**

Mark one answer

- [ ] **A.** you can see well ahead that the hard shoulder is clear
- [ ] **B.** the traffic in the right-hand lane is signalling right
- [ ] **C.** you warn drivers behind by signalling left
- [ ] **D.** there is a queue of slow-moving traffic to your right that is moving more slowly than you are

560 **You are towing a trailer on a motorway. What is your maximum speed limit?**

Mark one answer

- ☐ **A.** 40mph
- ☐ **B.** 50mph
- ☐ **C.** 60mph
- ☐ **D.** 70mph

561 **The left-hand lane of a motorway should be used for**

Mark one answer

- ☐ **A.** breakdowns and emergencies only
- ☐ **B.** overtaking slower traffic in the other lanes
- ☐ **C.** slow vehicles only
- ☐ **D.** normal driving

562 **You are driving on a motorway. You have to slow down quickly due to a hazard. You should**

Mark one answer

- ☐ **A.** switch on your hazard lights
- ☐ **B.** switch on your headlights
- ☐ **C.** sound your horn
- ☐ **D.** flash your headlights

563 **You get a puncture on the motorway. You manage to get your vehicle on to the hard shoulder. You should**

Mark one answer

- ☐ **A.** change the wheel yourself immediately
- ☐ **B.** use the emergency telephone and call for assistance
- ☐ **C.** try to wave down another vehicle for help
- ☐ **D.** only change the wheel if you have a passenger to help you

564 **You are driving on a motorway. By mistake, you go past the exit that you wanted to take. You should**

Mark one answer

- ☐ **A.** carefully reverse on the hard shoulder
- ☐ **B.** carry on to the next exit
- ☐ **C.** carefully reverse in the left-hand lane
- ☐ **D.** make a U-turn at the next gap in the central reservation

565 **Your vehicle breaks down on the hard shoulder of a motorway. You decide to use your mobile phone to call for help. You should**

Mark one answer

- ☐ **A.** stand at the rear of the vehicle while making the call
- ☐ **B.** try to repair the vehicle yourself
- ☐ **C.** get out of the vehicle by the right-hand door
- ☐ **D.** check your location from the marker posts on the left

566 **You are travelling on a motorway. Unless signs show a lower speed limit you must NOT exceed**

Mark one answer **NI**

- ☐ **A.** 50mph
- ☐ **B.** 60mph
- ☐ **C.** 70mph
- ☐ **D.** 80mph

567 **You are on a three-lane motorway towing a trailer. You may use the right-hand lane when**

Mark one answer **NI**

- ☐ **A.** there are lane closures
- ☐ **B.** there is slow-moving traffic
- ☐ **C.** you can maintain a high speed
- ☐ **D.** large vehicles are in the left and centre lanes

568

You are on a motorway. There is a contraflow system ahead. What would you expect to find?

Mark one answer

- ☐ **A.** Temporary traffic lights
- ☐ **B.** Lower speed limits
- ☐ **C.** Wider lanes than normal
- ☐ **D.** Speed humps

569

You are driving at 70mph on a three-lane motorway. There is no traffic ahead. Which lane should you use?

Mark one answer

- ☐ **A.** Any lane
- ☐ **B.** Middle lane
- ☐ **C.** Right lane
- ☐ **D.** Left lane

570

Your vehicle has broken down on a motorway. You are not able to stop on the hard shoulder. What should you do?

Mark one answer

- ☐ **A.** Switch on your hazard warning lights
- ☐ **B.** Stop following traffic and ask for help
- ☐ **C.** Attempt to repair your vehicle quickly
- ☐ **D.** Stand behind your vehicle to warn others

571

Why is it particularly important to carry out a check on your vehicle before making a long motorway journey?

Mark one answer

- ☐ **A.** You will have to do more harsh braking on motorways
- ☐ **B.** Motorway service stations do not deal with breakdowns
- ☐ **C.** The road surface will wear down the tyres faster
- ☐ **D.** Continuous high speeds may increase the risk of your vehicle breaking down

572

For what reason may you use the right-hand lane of a motorway?

Mark one answer

- ☐ **A.** For keeping out of the way of lorries
- ☐ **B.** For travelling at more than 70mph
- ☐ **C.** For turning right
- ☐ **D.** For overtaking other vehicles

573

On a motorway you may ONLY stop on the hard shoulder

Mark one answer

- ☐ **A.** in an emergency
- ☐ **B.** if you feel tired and need to rest
- ☐ **C.** if you accidentally go past the exit that you wanted to take
- ☐ **D.** to pick up a hitchhiker

574 **You are driving on a motorway. The car ahead shows its hazard lights for a short time. This tells you that**

Mark one answer

- [ ] **A.** the driver wants you to overtake
- [ ] **B.** the other car is going to change lanes
- [ ] **C.** traffic ahead is slowing or stopping suddenly
- [ ] **D.** there is a police speed check ahead

575 **Motorway emergency telephones are usually linked to the police. In some areas they are now linked to**

Mark one answer

- [ ] **A.** the local ambulance service
- [ ] **B.** an Highways Agency control centre
- [ ] **C.** the local fire brigade
- [ ] **D.** a breakdown service control centre

576 **You are intending to leave the motorway at the next exit. Before you reach the exit you should normally position your vehicle**

Mark one answer

- [ ] **A.** in the middle lane
- [ ] **B.** in the left-hand lane
- [ ] **C.** on the hard shoulder
- [ ] **D.** in any lane

577 **As a provisional licence holder you should not drive a car**

Mark one answer

- [ ] **A.** over 30mph
- [ ] **B.** at night
- [ ] **C.** on the motorway
- [ ] **D.** with passengers in rear seats

578 **Motorway emergency telephones are usually linked to the police. In some areas they are now linked to**

Mark one answer **NI**

- [ ] **A.** the Highways Agency Control Centre
- [ ] **B.** the Driver Vehicle Licensing Agency
- [ ] **C.** the Driving Standards Agency
- [ ] **D.** the local Vehicle Registration Office

579 **An Emergency Refuge Area is an area**

Mark one answer

- [ ] **A.** on a motorway for use in cases of emergency or breakdown
- [ ] **B.** for use if you think you will be involved in a road rage incident
- [ ] **C.** on a motorway for a police patrol to park and watch traffic
- [ ] **D.** for construction and road workers to store emergency equipment

580 **What is an Emergency Refuge Area on a motorway for?**

Mark one answer

- [ ] **A.** An area to park in when you want to use a mobile phone
- [ ] **B.** To use in cases of emergency or breakdown
- [ ] **C.** For an emergency recovery vehicle to park in a contraflow system
- [ ] **D.** To drive in when there is queuing traffic ahead

581 **Highways Agency Traffic Officers**

Mark one answer **NI**

- [ ] **A.** will not be able to assist at a breakdown or emergency
- [ ] **B.** are not able to stop and direct anyone on a motorway
- [ ] **C.** will tow a broken down vehicle and its passengers home
- [ ] **D.** are able to stop and direct anyone on a motorway

582 **You are on a motorway. A red cross is displayed above the hard shoulder. What does this mean?**

Mark one answer NI

- [ ] **A.** Pull up in this lane to answer your mobile phone
- [ ] **B.** Use this lane as a running lane
- [ ] **C.** This lane can be used if you need a rest
- [ ] **D.** You should not travel in this lane

583 **You are on a motorway in an Active Traffic Management (ATM) area. A mandatory speed limit is displayed above the hard shoulder. What does this mean?**

Mark one answer NI

- [ ] **A.** You should not travel in this lane
- [ ] **B.** The hard shoulder can be used as a running lane
- [ ] **C.** You can park on the hard shoulder if you feel tired
- [ ] **D.** You can pull up in this lane to answer a mobile phone

584 **The aim of an Active Traffic Management scheme on a motorway is to**

Mark one answer NI

- [ ] **A.** prevent overtaking
- [ ] **B.** reduce rest stops
- [ ] **C.** prevent tailgating
- [ ] **D.** reduce congestion

585 **You are in an Active Traffic Management area on a motorway. When the Actively Managed mode is operating**

Mark one answer NI

- [ ] **A.** speed limits are only advisory
- [ ] **B.** the national speed limit will apply
- [ ] **C.** the speed limit is always 30mph
- [ ] **D.** all speed limit signals are set

586 **You are travelling on a motorway. A red cross is shown above the hard shoulder and mandatory speed limits above all other lanes. This means**

Mark one answer NI

- [ ] **A.** the hard shoulder can be used as a rest area if you feel tired
- [ ] **B.** the hard shoulder is for emergency or breakdown use only
- [ ] **C.** the hard shoulder can be used as a normal running lane
- [ ] **D.** the hard shoulder has a speed limit of 50mph

587

You are travelling on a motorway. A red cross is shown above the hard shoulder. What does this mean?

Mark one answer NI

- [ ] **A.** Use this lane as a rest area
- [ ] **B.** Use this as a normal running lane
- [ ] **C.** Do not use this lane to travel in
- [ ] **D.** National speed limit applies in this lane

588

You see this sign on a motorway. It means you can use

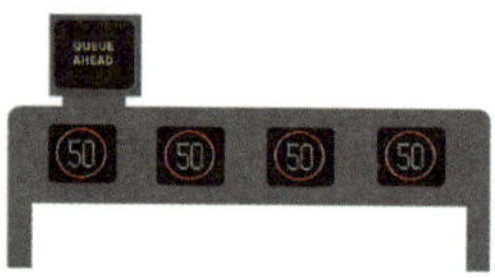

Mark one answer NI

- [ ] **A.** any lane except the hard shoulder
- [ ] **B.** the hard shoulder only
- [ ] **C.** the three right hand lanes only
- [ ] **D.** all the lanes including the hard shoulder

589

Why can it be an advantage for traffic speed to stay constant over a longer distance?

Mark one answer

- [ ] **A.** You will do more stop-start driving
- [ ] **B.** You will use far more fuel
- [ ] **C.** You will be able to use more direct routes
- [ ] **D.** Your overall journey time will normally improve

590

You should not normally travel on the hard shoulder of a motorway. When can you use it?

Mark one answer NI

- [ ] **A.** When taking the next exit
- [ ] **B.** When traffic is stopped
- [ ] **C.** When signs direct you to
- [ ] **D.** When traffic is slow moving

591

On a motorway what is used to reduce traffic bunching?

Mark one answer

- [ ] **A.** Variable speed limits
- [ ] **B.** Contraflow systems
- [ ] **C.** National speed limits
- [ ] **D.** Lane closures

592

When may you stop on a motorway?

Mark one answer

- [ ] **A.** If you have to read a map
- [ ] **B.** When you are tired and need a rest
- [ ] **C.** If your mobile phone rings
- [ ] **D.** In an emergency or breakdown

593 **What is the meaning of this sign?**

Mark one answer

- [ ] **A.** Local speed limit applies
- [ ] **B.** No waiting on the carriageway
- [ ] **C.** National speed limit applies
- [ ] **D.** No entry to vehicular traffic

594 **What is the national speed limit on a single carriageway road for cars and motorcycles?**

Mark one answer

- [ ] **A.** 30mph
- [ ] **B.** 50mph
- [ ] **C.** 60mph
- [ ] **D.** 70mph

595 **What is the national speed limit for cars and motorcycles on a dual carriageway?**

Mark one answer

- [ ] **A.** 30mph
- [ ] **B.** 50mph
- [ ] **C.** 60mph
- [ ] **D.** 70mph

596 **There are no speed limit signs on the road. How is a 30mph limit indicated?**

Mark one answer

- [ ] **A.** By hazard warning lines
- [ ] **B.** By street lighting
- [ ] **C.** By pedestrian islands
- [ ] **D.** By double or single yellow lines

597 **Where you see street lights but no speed limit signs the limit is usually**

Mark one answer

- [ ] **A.** 30mph
- [ ] **B.** 40mph
- [ ] **C.** 50mph
- [ ] **D.** 60mph

598 **What does this sign mean?**

Mark one answer

- [ ] **A.** Minimum speed 30mph
- [ ] **B.** End of maximum speed
- [ ] **C.** End of minimum speed
- [ ] **D.** Maximum speed 30mph

599 **There is a tractor ahead of you. You wish to overtake but you are NOT sure if it is safe to do so. You should**

Mark one answer

- [ ] **A.** follow another overtaking vehicle through
- [ ] **B.** sound your horn to the slow vehicle to pull over
- [ ] **C.** speed through but flash your lights to oncoming traffic
- [ ] **D.** not overtake if you are in doubt

600 Which three of the following are most likely to take an unusual course at roundabouts?

Mark three answers

- [ ] **A.** Horse riders
- [ ] **B.** Milk floats
- [ ] **C.** Delivery vans
- [ ] **D.** Long vehicles
- [ ] **E.** Estate cars
- [ ] **F.** Cyclists

601 In which TWO places should you NOT park?

Mark two answers

- [ ] **A.** Near a school entrance
- [ ] **B.** Near a police station
- [ ] **C.** In a side road
- [ ] **D.** At a bus stop
- [ ] **E.** In a one-way street

602 On a clearway you must not stop

Mark one answer

- [ ] **A.** at any time
- [ ] **B.** when it is busy
- [ ] **C.** in the rush hour
- [ ] **D.** during daylight hours

603 What is the meaning of this sign?

Mark one answer

- [ ] **A.** No entry
- [ ] **B.** Waiting restrictions
- [ ] **C.** National speed limit
- [ ] **D.** School crossing patrol

604 You can park on the right-hand side of a road at night

Mark one answer

- [ ] **A.** in a one-way street
- [ ] **B.** with your sidelights on
- [ ] **C.** more than 10 metres (32 feet) from a junction
- [ ] **D.** under a lamppost

605 On a three-lane dual carriageway the right-hand lane can be used for

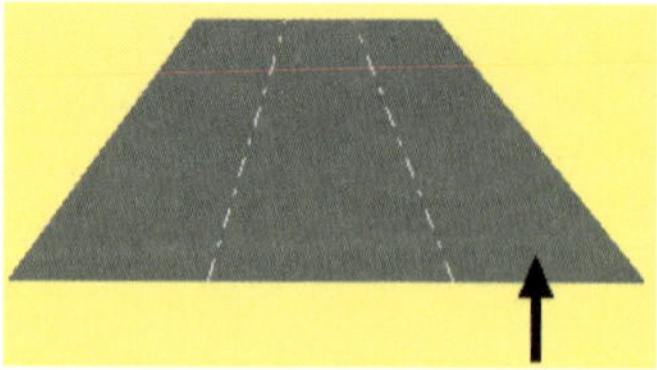

Mark one answer

- [ ] **A.** overtaking only, never turning right
- [ ] **B.** overtaking or turning right
- [ ] **C.** fast-moving traffic only
- [ ] **D.** turning right only, never overtaking

606 You are approaching a busy junction. There are several lanes with road markings. At the last moment you realise that you are in the wrong lane. You should

Mark one answer

- [ ] **A.** continue in that lane
- [ ] **B.** force your way across
- [ ] **C.** stop until the area has cleared
- [ ] **D.** use clear arm signals to cut across

607 Where may you overtake on a one-way street?

Mark one answer

- [ ] **A.** Only on the left-hand side
- [ ] **B.** Overtaking is not allowed
- [ ] **C.** Only on the right-hand side
- [ ] **D.** Either on the right or the left

608 When going straight ahead at a roundabout you should

Mark one answer

- [ ] **A.** indicate left before leaving the roundabout
- [ ] **B.** not indicate at any time
- [ ] **C.** indicate right when approaching the roundabout
- [ ] **D.** indicate left when approaching the roundabout

609 Which vehicle might have to use a different course to normal at roundabouts?

Mark one answer

- [ ] **A.** Sports car
- [ ] **B.** Van
- [ ] **C.** Estate car
- [ ] **D.** Long vehicle

610 You are going straight ahead at a roundabout. How should you signal?

Mark one answer

- [ ] **A.** Signal right on the approach and then left to leave the roundabout
- [ ] **B.** Signal left as you leave the roundabout
- [ ] **C.** Signal left on the approach to the roundabout and keep the signal on until you leave
- [ ] **D.** Signal left just after you pass the exit before the one you will take

611 You may only enter a box junction when

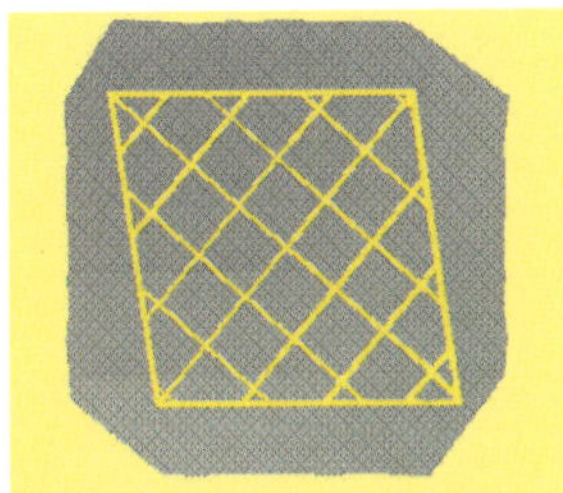

Mark one answer

- [ ] **A.** there are less than two vehicles in front of you
- [ ] **B.** the traffic lights show green
- [ ] **C.** your exit road is clear
- [ ] **D.** you need to turn left

612 You may wait in a yellow box junction when

Mark one answer

- [ ] **A.** oncoming traffic is preventing you from turning right
- [ ] **B.** you are in a queue of traffic turning left
- [ ] **C.** you are in a queue of traffic to go ahead
- [ ] **D.** you are on a roundabout

613 You MUST stop when signalled to do so by which THREE of these?

Mark three answers

- [ ] **A.** A police officer
- [ ] **B.** A pedestrian
- [ ] **C.** A school crossing patrol
- [ ] **D.** A bus driver
- [ ] **E.** A red traffic light

614 You will see these red and white markers when approaching

Mark one answer

- [ ] **A.** the end of a motorway
- [ ] **B.** a concealed level crossing
- [ ] **C.** a concealed speed limit sign
- [ ] **D.** the end of a dual carriageway

615 Someone is waiting to cross at a zebra crossing. They are standing on the pavement. You should normally

Mark one answer

- [ ] **A.** go on quickly before they step on to the crossing
- [ ] **B.** stop before you reach the zigzag lines and let them cross
- [ ] **C.** stop, let them cross, wait patiently
- [ ] **D.** ignore them as they are still on the pavement

616 At toucan crossings, apart from pedestrians you should be aware of

Mark one answer

- [ ] **A.** emergency vehicles emerging
- [ ] **B.** buses pulling out
- [ ] **C.** trams crossing in front
- [ ] **D.** cyclists riding across

617 Who can use a toucan crossing?

Mark two answers

- [ ] **A.** Trains
- [ ] **B.** Cyclists
- [ ] **C.** Buses
- [ ] **D.** Pedestrians
- [ ] **E.** Trams

618 At a pelican crossing, what does a flashing amber light mean?

Mark one answer

- [ ] **A.** You must not move off until the lights stop flashing
- [ ] **B.** You must give way to pedestrians still on the crossing
- [ ] **C.** You can move off, even if pedestrians are still on the crossing
- [ ] **D.** You must stop because the lights are about to change to red

619 You are waiting at a pelican crossing. The red light changes to flashing amber. This means you must

Mark one answer

- [ ] **A.** wait for pedestrians on the crossing to clear
- [ ] **B.** move off immediately without any hesitation
- [ ] **C.** wait for the green light before moving off
- [ ] **D.** get ready and go when the continuous amber light shows

620 You are travelling on a well-lit road at night in a built-up area. By using dipped headlights you will be able to

Mark one answer

- [ ] **A.** see further along the road
- [ ] **B.** go at a much faster speed
- [ ] **C.** switch to main beam quickly
- [ ] **D.** be easily seen by others

621 When can you park on the left opposite these road markings?

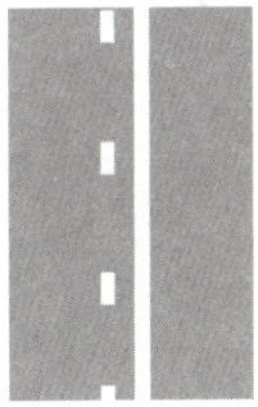

Mark one answer

- [ ] **A.** If the line nearest to you is broken
- [ ] **B.** When there are no yellow lines
- [ ] **C.** To pick up or set down passengers
- [ ] **D.** During daylight hours only

622 You are intending to turn right at a crossroads. An oncoming driver is also turning right. It will normally be safer to

Mark one answer

- [ ] **A.** keep the other vehicle to your RIGHT and turn behind it (offside to offside)
- [ ] **B.** keep the other vehicle to your LEFT and turn in front of it (nearside to nearside)
- [ ] **C.** carry on and turn at the next junction instead
- [ ] **D.** hold back and wait for the other driver to turn first

623 You are on a road that has no traffic signs. There are street lights. What is the speed limit?

Mark one answer

- [ ] **A.** 20mph
- [ ] **B.** 30mph
- [ ] **C.** 40mph
- [ ] **D.** 60mph

624 **You are going along a street with parked vehicles on the left-hand side. For which THREE reasons should you keep your speed down?**

Mark three answers
- [ ] **A.** So that oncoming traffic can see you more clearly
- [ ] **B.** You may set off car alarms
- [ ] **C.** Vehicles may be pulling out
- [ ] **D.** Drivers' doors may open
- [ ] **E.** Children may run out from between the vehicles

625 **You meet an obstruction on your side of the road. You should**

Mark one answer
- [ ] **A.** carry on, you have priority
- [ ] **B.** give way to oncoming traffic
- [ ] **C.** wave oncoming vehicles through
- [ ] **D.** accelerate to get past first

626 **You are on a two-lane dual carriageway. For which TWO of the following would you use the right-hand lane?**

Mark two answers
- [ ] **A.** Turning right
- [ ] **B.** Normal progress
- [ ] **C.** Staying at the minimum allowed speed
- [ ] **D.** Constant high speed
- [ ] **E.** Overtaking slower traffic
- [ ] **F.** Mending punctures

627 **Who has priority at an unmarked crossroads?**

Mark one answer
- [ ] **A.** The larger vehicle
- [ ] **B.** No one has priority
- [ ] **C.** The faster vehicle
- [ ] **D.** The smaller vehicle

628 **What is the nearest you may park to a junction?**

Mark one answer **NI**
- [ ] **A.** 10 metres (32 feet)
- [ ] **B.** 12 metres (39 feet)
- [ ] **C.** 15 metres (49 feet)
- [ ] **D.** 20 metres (66 feet)

629 **In which THREE places must you NOT park?**

Mark three answers **NI**
- [ ] **A.** Near the brow of a hill
- [ ] **B.** At or near a bus stop
- [ ] **C.** Where there is no pavement
- [ ] **D.** Within 10 metres (32 feet) of a junction
- [ ] **E.** On a 40mph road

630 **You are waiting at a level crossing. A train has passed but the lights keep flashing. You must**

Mark one answer
- [ ] **A.** carry on waiting
- [ ] **B.** phone the signal operator
- [ ] **C.** edge over the stop line and look for trains
- [ ] **D.** park and investigate

631 You park at night on a road with a 40mph speed limit. You should park

Mark one answer

- [ ] **A.** facing the traffic
- [ ] **B.** with parking lights on
- [ ] **C.** with dipped headlights on
- [ ] **D.** near a street light

632 The dual carriageway you are turning right on to has a very narrow central reservation. What should you do?

Mark one answer

- [ ] **A.** Proceed to the central reservation and wait
- [ ] **B.** Wait until the road is clear in both directions
- [ ] **C.** Stop in the first lane so that other vehicles give way
- [ ] **D.** Emerge slightly to show your intentions

633 At a crossroads there are no signs or road markings. Two vehicles approach. Which has priority?

Mark one answer

- [ ] **A.** Neither of the vehicles
- [ ] **B.** The vehicle travelling the fastest
- [ ] **C.** Oncoming vehicles turning right
- [ ] **D.** Vehicles approaching from the right

634 What does this sign tell you?

Mark one answer

- [ ] **A.** That it is a no-through road
- [ ] **B.** End of traffic calming zone
- [ ] **C.** Free parking zone ends
- [ ] **D.** No waiting zone ends

635 You are entering an area of road works. There is a temporary speed limit displayed. You should

Mark one answer

- [ ] **A.** not exceed the speed limit
- [ ] **B.** obey the limit only during rush hour
- [ ] **C.** ignore the displayed limit
- [ ] **D.** obey the limit except at night

636 You may drive over a footpath

Mark one answer

- [ ] **A.** to overtake slow-moving traffic
- [ ] **B.** when the pavement is very wide
- [ ] **C.** if no pedestrians are near
- [ ] **D.** to get into a property

637 A single-carriageway road has this sign. What is the maximum permitted speed for a car towing a trailer?

Mark one answer
- [ ] **A.** 30mph
- [ ] **B.** 40mph
- [ ] **C.** 50mph
- [ ] **D.** 60mph

638 You are towing a small caravan on a dual carriageway. You must not exceed

Mark one answer
- [ ] **A.** 50mph
- [ ] **B.** 40mph
- [ ] **C.** 70mph
- [ ] **D.** 60mph

639 You want to park and you see this sign. On the days and times shown you should

Mark one answer
- [ ] **A.** park in a bay and not pay
- [ ] **B.** park on yellow lines and pay
- [ ] **C.** park on yellow lines and not pay
- [ ] **D.** park in a bay and pay

640 As a car driver which THREE lanes are you NOT normally allowed to use?

Mark three answers
- [ ] **A.** Crawler lane
- [ ] **B.** Bus lane
- [ ] **C.** Overtaking lane
- [ ] **D.** Acceleration lane
- [ ] **E.** Cycle lane
- [ ] **F.** Tram lane

641 You are driving along a road that has a cycle lane. The lane is marked by a solid white line. This means that during its period of operation

Mark one answer
- [ ] **A.** the lane may be used for parking your car
- [ ] **B.** you may drive in that lane at any time
- [ ] **C.** the lane may be used when necessary
- [ ] **D.** you must not drive in that lane

642 A cycle lane is marked by a solid white line. You must not drive or park in it

Mark one answer
- [ ] **A.** at any time
- [ ] **B.** during the rush hour
- [ ] **C.** if a cyclist is using it
- [ ] **D.** during its period of operation

643 While driving, you intend to turn left into a minor road. On the approach you should

Mark one answer
- [ ] **A.** keep just left of the middle of the road
- [ ] **B.** keep in the middle of the road
- [ ] **C.** swing out wide just before turning
- [ ] **D.** keep well to the left of the road

644 **You are waiting at a level crossing. The red warning lights continue to flash after a train has passed by. What should you do?**

Mark one answer
- [ ] **A.** Get out and investigate
- [ ] **B.** Telephone the signal operator
- [ ] **C.** Continue to wait
- [ ] **D.** Drive across carefully

645 **You are driving over a level crossing. The warning lights come on and a bell rings. What should you do?**

Mark one answer
- [ ] **A.** Get everyone out of the vehicle immediately
- [ ] **B.** Stop and reverse back to clear the crossing
- [ ] **C.** Keep going and clear the crossing
- [ ] **D.** Stop immediately and use your hazard warning lights

646 **You are on a busy main road and find that you are travelling in the wrong direction. What should you do?**

Mark one answer
- [ ] **A.** Turn into a side road on the right and reverse into the main road
- [ ] **B.** Make a U-turn in the main road
- [ ] **C.** Make a 'three-point' turn in the main road
- [ ] **D.** Turn round in a side road

647 **You may remove your seat belt when carrying out a manoeuvre that involves**

Mark one answer
- [ ] **A.** reversing
- [ ] **B.** a hill start
- [ ] **C.** an emergency stop
- [ ] **D.** driving slowly

648 **You must not reverse**

Mark one answer
- [ ] **A.** for longer than necessary
- [ ] **B.** for more than a car's length
- [ ] **C.** into a side road
- [ ] **D.** in a built-up area

649 **You are parked in a busy high street. What is the safest way to turn your vehicle around so you can go the opposite way?**

Mark one answer
- [ ] **A.** Find a quiet side road to turn round in
- [ ] **B.** Drive into a side road and reverse into the main road
- [ ] **C.** Get someone to stop the traffic
- [ ] **D.** Do a U-turn

650 **When you are NOT sure that it is safe to reverse your vehicle you should**

Mark one answer

- [ ] **A.** use your horn
- [ ] **B.** rev your engine
- [ ] **C.** get out and check
- [ ] **D.** reverse slowly

651 **When may you reverse from a side road into a main road?**

Mark one answer

- [ ] **A.** Only if both roads are clear of traffic
- [ ] **B.** Not at any time
- [ ] **C.** At any time
- [ ] **D.** Only if the main road is clear of traffic

652 **You want to turn right at a box junction. There is oncoming traffic. You should**

Mark one answer

- [ ] **A.** wait in the box junction if your exit is clear
- [ ] **B.** wait before the junction until it is clear of all traffic
- [ ] **C.** drive on, you cannot turn right at a box junction
- [ ] **D.** drive slowly into the box junction when signalled by oncoming traffic

653 **You are reversing your vehicle into a side road. When would the greatest hazard to passing traffic occur?**

Mark one answer

- [ ] **A.** After you've completed the manoeuvre
- [ ] **B.** Just before you actually begin to manoeuvre
- [ ] **C.** After you've entered the side road
- [ ] **D.** When the front of your vehicle swings out

654 **You are driving on a road that has a cycle lane. The lane is marked by a broken white line. This means that**

Mark two answers

- [ ] **A.** you should not drive in the lane unless it is unavoidable
- [ ] **B.** you should not park in the lane unless it is unavoidable
- [ ] **C.** cyclists can travel in both directions in that lane
- [ ] **D.** the lane must be used by motorcyclists in heavy traffic

655 **Where is the safest place to park your vehicle at night?**

Mark one answer

- [ ] **A.** In a garage
- [ ] **B.** On a busy road
- [ ] **C.** In a quiet car park
- [ ] **D.** Near a red route

656 **To help keep your vehicle secure at night where should you park?**

Mark one answer

- [ ] **A.** Near a police station
- [ ] **B.** In a quiet road
- [ ] **C.** On a red route
- [ ] **D.** In a well-lit area

657

You are in the right-hand lane of a dual carriageway. You see signs showing that the right-hand lane is closed 800 yards ahead. You should

Mark one answer

- [ ] **A.** keep in that lane until you reach the queue
- [ ] **B.** move to the left immediately
- [ ] **C.** wait and see which lane is moving faster
- [ ] **D.** move to the left in good time

658

You are driving on an urban clearway. You may stop only to

Mark one answer

- [ ] **A.** set down and pick up passengers
- [ ] **B.** use a mobile telephone
- [ ] **C.** ask for directions
- [ ] **D.** load or unload goods

659

You are looking for somewhere to park your vehicle. The area is full EXCEPT for spaces marked 'disabled use'. You can

Mark one answer

- [ ] **A.** use these spaces when elsewhere is full
- [ ] **B.** park if you stay with your vehicle
- [ ] **C.** use these spaces, disabled or not
- [ ] **D.** not park there unless permitted

660

Your vehicle is parked on the road at night. When must you use sidelights?

Mark one answer

- [ ] **A.** Where there are continuous white lines in the middle of the road
- [ ] **B.** Where the speed limit exceeds 30mph
- [ ] **C.** Where you are facing oncoming traffic
- [ ] **D.** Where you are near a bus stop

661

On which THREE occasions MUST you stop your vehicle?

Mark three answers

- [ ] **A.** When in an accident where damage or injury is caused
- [ ] **B.** At a red traffic light
- [ ] **C.** When signalled to do so by a police officer
- [ ] **D.** At a junction with double broken white lines
- [ ] **E.** At a pelican crossing when the amber light is flashing and no pedestrians are crossing

662

You are on a road that is only wide enough for one vehicle. There is a car coming towards you. What should you do?

Mark one answer

- [ ] **A.** Pull into a passing place on your right
- [ ] **B.** Force the other driver to reverse
- [ ] **C.** Pull into a passing place if your vehicle is wider
- [ ] **D.** Pull into a passing place on your left

663 What MUST you have to park in a disabled space?

Mark one answer

- [ ] **A.** An orange or blue badge
- [ ] **B.** A wheelchair
- [ ] **C.** An advanced driver certificate
- [ ] **D.** A modified vehicle

664 You are driving at night with full beam headlights on. A vehicle is overtaking you. You should dip your lights

Mark one answer

- [ ] **A.** some time after the vehicle has passed you
- [ ] **B.** before the vehicle starts to pass you
- [ ] **C.** only if the other driver dips their headlights
- [ ] **D.** as soon as the vehicle passes you

665 When may you drive a motor car in this bus lane?

Mark one answer

- [ ] **A.** Outside its hours of operation
- [ ] **B.** To get to the front of a traffic queue
- [ ] **C.** You may not use it at any time
- [ ] **D.** To overtake slow-moving traffic

666 Signals are normally given by direction indicators and

Mark one answer

- [ ] **A.** brake lights
- [ ] **B.** sidelights
- [ ] **C.** fog lights
- [ ] **D.** interior lights

667 You are travelling on a motorway. You MUST stop when signalled to do so by which of these?

Mark one answer **NI**

- [ ] **A.** Flashing amber lights above your lane
- [ ] **B.** A Highways Agency Traffic Officer
- [ ] **C.** Pedestrians on the hard shoulder
- [ ] **D.** A driver who has broken down

668 At a busy unmarked crossroads, which of the following has priority?

Mark one answer

- [ ] **A.** Vehicles going straight ahead
- [ ] **B.** Vehicles turning right
- [ ] **C.** None of the vehicles
- [ ] **D.** The vehicles that arrived first

669 You MUST obey signs giving orders. These signs are mostly in

Mark one answer

- [ ] **A.** green rectangles
- [ ] **B.** red triangles
- [ ] **C.** blue rectangles
- [ ] **D.** red circles

670 Traffic signs giving orders are generally which shape?

Mark one answer

- [ ] **A.**

- [ ] **B.**

- [ ] **C.**

- [ ] **D.**

671 Which type of sign tells you NOT to do something?

Mark one answer

- [ ] **A.**

- [ ] **B.**

- [ ] **C.**

- [ ] **D.**

672 What does this sign mean?

Mark one answer

- [ ] **A.** Maximum speed limit with traffic calming
- [ ] **B.** Minimum speed limit with traffic calming
- [ ] **C.** '20 cars only' parking zone
- [ ] **D.** Only 20 cars allowed at any one time

673 Which sign means no motor vehicles are allowed?

Mark one answer

- [ ] **A.**

- [ ] **B.**

- [ ] **C.**

- [ ] **D.**

674 Which of these signs means no motor vehicles?

Mark one answer

- [ ] **A.**

- [ ] **B.**

- [ ] **C.**

- [ ] **D.**

675 What does this sign mean?

Mark one answer

- [ ] **A.** New speed limit 20mph
- [ ] **B.** No vehicles over 30 tonnes
- [ ] **C.** Minimum speed limit 30mph
- [ ] **D.** End of 20mph zone

676 What does this sign mean?

Mark one answer

- [ ] **A.** No overtaking
- [ ] **B.** No motor vehicles
- [ ] **C.** Clearway (no stopping)
- [ ] **D.** Cars and motorcycles only

677 What does this sign mean?

Mark one answer

- [ ] **A.** No parking
- [ ] **B.** No road markings
- [ ] **C.** No through road
- [ ] **D.** No entry

678 What does this sign mean?

Mark one answer

- [ ] **A.** Bend to the right
- [ ] **B.** Road on the right closed
- [ ] **C.** No traffic from the right
- [ ] **D.** No right turn

679 Which sign means 'no entry'?

Mark one answer

- [ ] **A.**

- [ ] **B.**

- [ ] **C.**

- [ ] **D.**

680 What does this sign mean?

Mark one answer

- [ ] **A.** Route for trams only
- [ ] **B.** Route for buses only
- [ ] **C.** Parking for buses only
- [ ] **D.** Parking for trams only

681 Which type of vehicle does this sign apply to?

Mark one answer

- [ ] **A.** Wide vehicles
- [ ] **B.** Long vehicles
- [ ] **C.** High vehicles
- [ ] **D.** Heavy vehicles

682 Which sign means NO motor vehicles allowed?

Mark one answer

- [ ] **A.**

- [ ] **B.**

- [ ] **C.**

- [ ] **D.**

683 What does this sign mean?

Mark one answer

- [ ] **A.** You have priority
- [ ] **B.** No motor vehicles
- [ ] **C.** Two-way traffic
- [ ] **D.** No overtaking

684 What does this sign mean?

Mark one answer

- [ ] **A.** Keep in one lane
- [ ] **B.** Give way to oncoming traffic
- [ ] **C.** Do not overtake
- [ ] **D.** Form two lanes

685 Which sign means no overtaking?

Mark one answer

- [ ] **A.**

- [ ] **B.**

- [ ] **C.**

- [ ] **D.**

686 What does this sign mean?

Mark one answer

- [ ] **A.** Waiting restrictions apply
- [ ] **B.** Waiting permitted
- [ ] **C.** National speed limit applies
- [ ] **D.** Clearway (no stopping)

687 What does this sign mean?

Mark one answer

- [ ] **A.** End of restricted speed area
- [ ] **B.** End of restricted parking area
- [ ] **C.** End of clearway
- [ ] **D.** End of cycle route

688 Which sign means 'no stopping'?

Mark one answer

- [ ] **A.**

- [ ] **B.**

- [ ] **C.**

- [ ] **D.**

689 What does this sign mean?

Mark one answer

- [ ] **A.** Roundabout
- [ ] **B.** Crossroads
- [ ] **C.** No stopping
- [ ] **D.** No entry

690 You see this sign ahead. It means

Mark one answer

- [ ] **A.** national speed limit applies
- [ ] **B.** waiting restrictions apply
- [ ] **C.** no stopping
- [ ] **D.** no entry

691 What does this sign mean?

Mark one answer

- [ ] **A.** Distance to parking place ahead
- [ ] **B.** Distance to public telephone ahead
- [ ] **C.** Distance to public house ahead
- [ ] **D.** Distance to passing place ahead

692 What does this sign mean?

Mark one answer

- [ ] **A.** Vehicles may not park on the verge or footway
- [ ] **B.** Vehicles may park on the left-hand side of the road only
- [ ] **C.** Vehicles may park fully on the verge or footway
- [ ] **D.** Vehicles may park on the right-hand side of the road only

693 **What does this traffic sign mean?**

Mark one answer

- [ ] **A.** No overtaking allowed
- [ ] **B.** Give priority to oncoming traffic
- [ ] **C.** Two-way traffic
- [ ] **D.** One-way traffic only

694 **What is the meaning of this traffic sign?**

Mark one answer

- [ ] **A.** End of two-way road
- [ ] **B.** Give priority to vehicles coming towards you
- [ ] **C.** You have priority over vehicles coming towards you
- [ ] **D.** Bus lane ahead

695 **What MUST you do when you see this sign?**

Mark one answer

- [ ] **A.** Stop, only if traffic is approaching
- [ ] **B.** Stop, even if the road is clear
- [ ] **C.** Stop, only if children are waiting to cross
- [ ] **D.** Stop, only if a red light is showing

696 **What does this sign mean?**

Mark one answer

- [ ] **A.** No overtaking
- [ ] **B.** You are entering a one-way street
- [ ] **C.** Two-way traffic ahead
- [ ] **D.** You have priority over vehicles from the opposite direction

697 **What shape is a STOP sign at a junction?**

Mark one answer

- [ ] **A.**

- [ ] **B.**

- [ ] **C.**

- [ ] **D.**

698 **At a junction you see this sign partly covered by snow. What does it mean?**

Mark one answer

- [ ] **A.** Crossroads
- [ ] **B.** Give way
- [ ] **C.** Stop
- [ ] **D.** Turn right

699 Which shape is used for a 'give way' sign?

Mark one answer

☐ A.

☐ B.

☐ C.

☐ D.

700 What does this sign mean?

Mark one answer

☐ **A.** Service area 30 miles ahead
☐ **B.** Maximum speed 30mph
☐ **C.** Minimum speed 30mph
☐ **D.** Lay-by 30 miles ahead

701 Which of these signs means turn left ahead?

Mark one answer

☐ A.

☐ B.

☐ C.

☐ D.

702 What does this sign mean?

Mark one answer

☐ **A.** Buses turning
☐ **B.** Ring road
☐ **C.** Mini-roundabout
☐ **D.** Keep right

703 What does this sign mean?

Mark one answer

☐ **A.** Give way to oncoming vehicles
☐ **B.** Approaching traffic passes you on both sides
☐ **C.** Turn off at the next available junction
☐ **D.** Pass either side to get to the same destination

704 What does this sign mean?

Mark one answer

☐ **A.** Route for trams
☐ **B.** Give way to trams
☐ **C.** Route for buses
☐ **D.** Give way to buses

705 What does a circular traffic sign with a blue background do?

Mark one answer

- [ ] **A.** Give warning of a motorway ahead
- [ ] **B.** Give directions to a car park
- [ ] **C.** Give motorway information
- [ ] **D.** Give an instruction

706 Which of these signs means that you are entering a one-way street?

Mark one answer

- [ ] **A.**

- [ ] **B.**

- [ ] **C.**

- [ ] **D.**

707 Where would you see a contraflow bus and cycle lane?

Mark one answer

- [ ] **A.** On a dual carriageway
- [ ] **B.** On a roundabout
- [ ] **C.** On an urban motorway
- [ ] **D.** On a one-way street

708 What does this sign mean?

Mark one answer

- [ ] **A.** Bus station on the right
- [ ] **B.** Contraflow bus lane
- [ ] **C.** With-flow bus lane
- [ ] **D.** Give way to buses

709 What does this sign mean?

Mark one answer

- [ ] **A.** With-flow bus and cycle lane
- [ ] **B.** Contraflow bus and cycle lane
- [ ] **C.** No buses and cycles allowed
- [ ] **D.** No waiting for buses and cycles

710 What does a sign with a brown background show?

Mark one answer

- [ ] **A.** Tourist directions
- [ ] **B.** Primary roads
- [ ] **C.** Motorway routes
- [ ] **D.** Minor routes

711 This sign means

Mark one answer

- [ ] **A.** tourist attraction
- [ ] **B.** beware of trains
- [ ] **C.** level crossing
- [ ] **D.** beware of trams

712 What are triangular signs for?

Mark one answer

- [ ] **A.** To give warnings
- [ ] **B.** To give information
- [ ] **C.** To give orders
- [ ] **D.** To give directions

713 What does this sign mean?

Mark one answer

- [ ] **A.** Turn left ahead
- [ ] **B.** T-junction
- [ ] **C.** No through road
- [ ] **D.** Give way

714 What does this sign mean?

Mark one answer

- [ ] **A.** Multi-exit roundabout
- [ ] **B.** Risk of ice
- [ ] **C.** Six roads converge
- [ ] **D.** Place of historical interest

715 What does this sign mean?

Mark one answer

- [ ] **A.** Crossroads
- [ ] **B.** Level crossing with gate
- [ ] **C.** Level crossing without gate
- [ ] **D.** Ahead only

716 What does this sign mean?

Mark one answer

- [ ] **A.** Ring road
- [ ] **B.** Mini-roundabout
- [ ] **C.** No vehicles
- [ ] **D.** Roundabout

717 Which FOUR of these would be indicated by a triangular road sign?

Mark four answers

- [ ] **A.** Road narrows
- [ ] **B.** Ahead only
- [ ] **C.** Low bridge
- [ ] **D.** Minimum speed
- [ ] **E.** Children crossing
- [ ] **F.** T-junction

718 What does this sign mean?

Mark one answer

- [ ] **A.** Cyclists must dismount
- [ ] **B.** Cycles are not allowed
- [ ] **C.** Cycle route ahead
- [ ] **D.** Cycle in single file

719 Which sign means that pedestrians may be walking along the road?

Mark one answer

- [ ] **A.**

- [ ] **B.**

- [ ] **C.**

- [ ] **D.**

720 Which of these signs warn you of a pedestrian crossing?

Mark one answer

- [ ] **A.**

- [ ] **B.**

- [ ] **C.**

- [ ] **D.**

721 What does this sign mean?

Mark one answer

- [ ] **A.** No footpath ahead
- [ ] **B.** Pedestrians only ahead
- [ ] **C.** Pedestrian crossing ahead
- [ ] **D.** School crossing ahead

722 What does this sign mean?

Mark one answer

- [ ] **A.** School crossing patrol
- [ ] **B.** No pedestrians allowed
- [ ] **C.** Pedestrian zone – no vehicles
- [ ] **D.** Pedestrian crossing ahead

723 Which of these signs means there is a double bend ahead?

Mark one answer

- [ ] **A.**

- [ ] **B.**

- [ ] **C.**

- [ ] **D.**

724 What does this sign mean?

Mark one answer

- [ ] **A.** Wait at the barriers
- [ ] **B.** Wait at the crossroads
- [ ] **C.** Give way to trams
- [ ] **D.** Give way to farm vehicles

725 What does this sign mean?

Mark one answer

- [ ] **A.** Humpback bridge
- [ ] **B.** Humps in the road
- [ ] **C.** Entrance to tunnel
- [ ] **D.** Soft verges

726 What does this sign mean?

Mark one answer

- [ ] **A.** Low bridge ahead
- [ ] **B.** Tunnel ahead
- [ ] **C.** Ancient monument ahead
- [ ] **D.** Accident black spot ahead

727 What does this sign mean?

Mark one answer

- [ ] **A.** Two-way traffic straight ahead
- [ ] **B.** Two-way traffic crosses a one-way road
- [ ] **C.** Two-way traffic over a bridge
- [ ] **D.** Two-way traffic crosses a two-way road

728 Which sign means 'two-way traffic crosses a one-way road'?

Mark one answer

- [ ] **A.**

- [ ] **B.**

- [ ] **C.**

- [ ] **D.**

729 Which of these signs means the end of a dual carriageway?

Mark one answer

- [ ] **A.**

- [ ] **B.**

- [ ] **C.**

- [ ] **D.**

730 What does this sign mean?

Mark one answer

- [ ] **A.** End of dual carriageway
- [ ] **B.** Tall bridge
- [ ] **C.** Road narrows
- [ ] **D.** End of narrow bridge

731 What does this sign mean?

Mark one answer

- [ ] **A.** Two-way traffic ahead across a one-way road
- [ ] **B.** Traffic approaching you has priority
- [ ] **C.** Two-way traffic straight ahead
- [ ] **D.** Motorway contraflow system ahead

732 What does this sign mean?

Mark one answer

- [ ] **A.** Crosswinds
- [ ] **B.** Road noise
- [ ] **C.** Airport
- [ ] **D.** Adverse camber

733 What does this traffic sign mean?

Mark one answer

- [ ] **A.** Slippery road ahead
- [ ] **B.** Tyres liable to punctures ahead
- [ ] **C.** Danger ahead
- [ ] **D.** Service area ahead

734 You are about to overtake when you see this sign. You should

Mark one answer

- [ ] **A.** overtake the other driver as quickly as possible
- [ ] **B.** move to the right to get a better view
- [ ] **C.** switch your headlights on before overtaking
- [ ] **D.** hold back until you can see clearly ahead

735 What does this sign mean?

Mark one answer

- ☐ **A.** Level crossing with gate or barrier
- ☐ **B.** Gated road ahead
- ☐ **C.** Level crossing without gate or barrier
- ☐ **D.** Cattle grid ahead

736 What does this sign mean?

Mark one answer

- ☐ **A.** No trams ahead
- ☐ **B.** Oncoming trams
- ☐ **C.** Trams crossing ahead
- ☐ **D.** Trams only

737 What does this sign mean?

Mark one answer

- ☐ **A.** Adverse camber
- ☐ **B.** Steep hill downwards
- ☐ **C.** Uneven road
- ☐ **D.** Steep hill upwards

738 What does this sign mean?

Mark one answer

- ☐ **A.** Uneven road surface
- ☐ **B.** Bridge over the road
- ☐ **C.** Road ahead ends
- ☐ **D.** Water across the road

739 What does this sign mean?

Mark one answer

- ☐ **A.** Humpback bridge
- ☐ **B.** Traffic calming hump
- ☐ **C.** Low bridge
- ☐ **D.** Uneven road

740 What does this sign mean?

Mark one answer

- ☐ **A.** Turn left for parking area
- ☐ **B.** No through road on the left
- ☐ **C.** No entry for traffic turning left
- ☐ **D.** Turn left for ferry terminal

741 What does this sign mean?

Mark one answer

- [ ] **A.** T-junction
- [ ] **B.** No through road
- [ ] **C.** Telephone box ahead
- [ ] **D.** Toilet ahead

742 Which sign means 'no through road'?

Mark one answer

- [ ] **A.**

- [ ] **B.**

- [ ] **C.**

- [ ] **D.**

743 Which of the following signs informs you that you are coming to a 'no through road'?

Mark one answer

- [ ] **A.**

- [ ] **B.**

- [ ] **C.**

- [ ] **D.**

744 What does this sign mean?

Mark one answer

- [ ] **A.** Direction to park-and-ride car park
- [ ] **B.** No parking for buses or coaches
- [ ] **C.** Directions to bus and coach park
- [ ] **D.** Parking area for cars and coaches

745 You are in a tunnel and you see this sign. What does it mean?

Mark one answer

- [ ] **A.** Direction to emergency pedestrian exit
- [ ] **B.** Beware of pedestrians, no footpath ahead
- [ ] **C.** No access for pedestrians
- [ ] **D.** Beware of pedestrians crossing ahead

746 Which is the sign for a ring road?

Mark one answer

- [ ] **A.**

- [ ] **B.**

- [ ] **C.**

- [ ] **D.**

747 At a railway level crossing the red light signal continues to flash after a train has gone by. What should you do?

Mark one answer

- [ ] A. Phone the signal operator
- [ ] B. Alert drivers behind you
- [ ] C. Wait
- [ ] D. Proceed with caution

748 At a junction you see this signal. It means

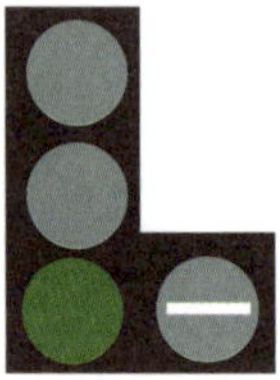

Mark one answer

- [ ] A. cars must stop
- [ ] B. trams must stop
- [ ] C. both trams and cars must stop
- [ ] D. both trams and cars can continue

749 What does this sign mean?

Mark one answer

- [ ] A. The right-hand lane ahead is narrow
- [ ] B. Right-hand lane for buses only
- [ ] C. Right-hand lane for turning right
- [ ] D. The right-hand lane is closed

750 What does this sign mean?

Mark one answer

- [ ] A. Change to the left lane
- [ ] B. Leave at the next exit
- [ ] C. Contraflow system
- [ ] D. One-way street

751 What does this sign mean?

Mark one answer

- [ ] A. Leave motorway at next exit
- [ ] B. Lane for heavy and slow vehicles
- [ ] C. All lorries use the hard shoulder
- [ ] D. Rest area for lorries

752 You are approaching a red traffic light. The signal will change from red to

Mark one answer

- [ ] **A.** red and amber, then green
- [ ] **B.** green, then amber
- [ ] **C.** amber, then green
- [ ] **D.** green and amber, then green

753 A red traffic light means

Mark one answer

- [ ] **A.** you should stop unless turning left
- [ ] **B.** stop, if you are able to brake safely
- [ ] **C.** you must stop and wait behind the stop line
- [ ] **D.** proceed with caution

754 At traffic lights, amber on its own means

Mark one answer

- [ ] **A.** prepare to go
- [ ] **B.** go if the way is clear
- [ ] **C.** go if no pedestrians are crossing
- [ ] **D.** stop at the stop line

755 You are approaching traffic lights. Red and amber are showing. This means

Mark one answer

- [ ] **A.** pass the lights if the road is clear
- [ ] **B.** there is a fault with the lights – take care
- [ ] **C.** wait for the green light before you cross the stop line
- [ ] **D.** the lights are about to change to red

756 You are at a junction controlled by traffic lights. When should you NOT proceed at green?

Mark one answer

- [ ] **A.** When pedestrians are waiting to cross
- [ ] **B.** When your exit from the junction is blocked
- [ ] **C.** When you think the lights may be about to change
- [ ] **D.** When you intend to turn right

757 You are in the left-hand lane at traffic lights. You are waiting to turn left. At which of these traffic lights must you NOT move on?

Mark one answer

- [ ] **A.**

- [ ] **B.**

- [ ] **C.**

- [ ] **D.**

758 What does this sign mean?

Mark one answer

- [ ] **A.** Traffic lights out of order
- [ ] **B.** Amber signal out of order
- [ ] **C.** Temporary traffic lights ahead
- [ ] **D.** New traffic lights ahead

759 When traffic lights are out of order, who has priority?

Mark one answer

- [ ] **A.** Traffic going straight on
- [ ] **B.** Traffic turning right
- [ ] **C.** Nobody
- [ ] **D.** Traffic turning left

760 These flashing red lights mean STOP. In which THREE of the following places could you find them?

Mark three answers

- [ ] **A.** Pelican crossings
- [ ] **B.** Lifting bridges
- [ ] **C.** Zebra crossings
- [ ] **D.** Level crossings
- [ ] **E.** Motorway exits
- [ ] **F.** Fire stations

761 What do these zigzag lines at pedestrian crossings mean?

Mark one answer

- [ ] **A.** No parking at any time
- [ ] **B.** Parking allowed only for a short time
- [ ] **C.** Slow down to 20mph
- [ ] **D.** Sounding horns is not allowed

762 When may you cross a double solid white line in the middle of the road?

Mark one answer

- [ ] **A.** To pass traffic that is queuing back at a junction
- [ ] **B.** To pass a car signalling to turn left ahead
- [ ] **C.** To pass a road maintenance vehicle travelling at 10mph or less
- [ ] **D.** To pass a vehicle that is towing a trailer

763 What does this road marking mean?

Mark one answer

- [ ] **A.** Do not cross the line
- [ ] **B.** No stopping allowed
- [ ] **C.** You are approaching a hazard
- [ ] **D.** No overtaking allowed

764 This marking appears on the road just before a

Mark one answer

- [ ] **A.** 'no entry' sign
- [ ] **B.** 'give way' sign
- [ ] **C.** 'stop' sign
- [ ] **D.** 'no through road' sign

765 Where would you see this road marking?

Mark one answer

- [ ] **A.** At traffic lights
- [ ] **B.** On road humps
- [ ] **C.** Near a level crossing
- [ ] **D.** At a box junction

766 Which is a hazard warning line?

Mark one answer

- [ ] **A.**

- [ ] **B.**

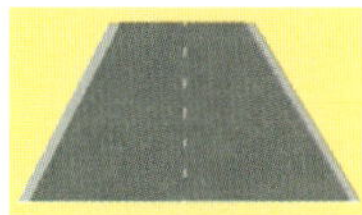

- [ ] **C.**

- [ ] **D.**

767 At this junction there is a stop sign with a solid white line on the road surface. Why is there a stop sign here?

Mark one answer

- [ ] **A.** Speed on the major road is de-restricted
- [ ] **B.** It is a busy junction
- [ ] **C.** Visibility along the major road is restricted
- [ ] **D.** There are hazard warning lines in the centre of the road

768 You see this line across the road at the entrance to a roundabout. What does it mean?

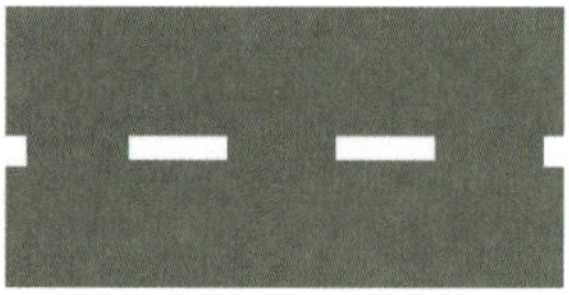

Mark one answer
- [ ] **A.** Give way to traffic from the right
- [ ] **B.** Traffic from the left has right of way
- [ ] **C.** You have right of way
- [ ] **D.** Stop at the line

769 Where would you find these road markings?

Mark one answer
- [ ] **A.** At a railway crossing
- [ ] **B.** At a junction
- [ ] **C.** On a motorway
- [ ] **D.** On a pedestrian crossing

770 How will a police officer in a patrol vehicle normally get you to stop?

Mark one answer
- [ ] **A.** Flash the headlights, indicate left and point to the left
- [ ] **B.** Wait until you stop, then approach you
- [ ] **C.** Use the siren, overtake, cut in front and stop
- [ ] **D.** Pull alongside you, use the siren and wave you to stop

771 There is a police car following you. The police officer flashes the headlights and points to the left. What should you do?

Mark one answer
- [ ] **A.** Turn left at the next junction
- [ ] **B.** Pull up on the left
- [ ] **C.** Stop immediately
- [ ] **D.** Move over to the left

772 You approach a junction. The traffic lights are not working. A police officer gives this signal. You should

Mark one answer
- [ ] **A.** turn left only
- [ ] **B.** turn right only
- [ ] **C.** stop level with the officer's arm
- [ ] **D.** stop at the stop line

773 The driver of the car in front is giving this arm signal. What does it mean?

Mark one answer
- [ ] **A.** The driver is slowing down
- [ ] **B.** The driver intends to turn right
- [ ] **C.** The driver wishes to overtake
- [ ] **D.** The driver intends to turn left

774 Where would you see these road markings?

Mark one answer

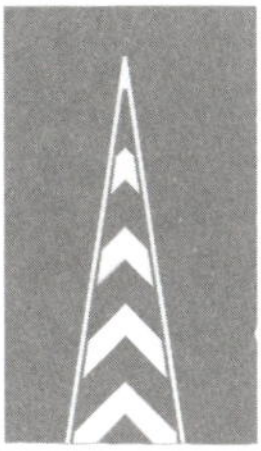

- [ ] **A.** At a level crossing
- [ ] **B.** On a motorway slip road
- [ ] **C.** At a pedestrian crossing
- [ ] **D.** On a single-track road

775 When may you NOT overtake on the left?

Mark one answer

- [ ] **A.** On a free-flowing motorway or dual carriageway
- [ ] **B.** When the traffic is moving slowly in queues
- [ ] **C.** On a one-way street
- [ ] **D.** When the car in front is signalling to turn right

776 What does this motorway sign mean?

Mark one answer

- [ ] **A.** Change to the lane on your left
- [ ] **B.** Leave the motorway at the next exit
- [ ] **C.** Change to the opposite carriageway
- [ ] **D.** Pull up on the hard shoulder

777 What does this motorway sign mean?

Mark one answer

- [ ] **A.** Temporary minimum speed 50mph
- [ ] **B.** No services for 50 miles
- [ ] **C.** Obstruction 50 metres (164 feet) ahead
- [ ] **D.** Temporary maximum speed 50mph

778 What does this sign mean?

Mark one answer

- [ ] **A.** Through traffic to use left lane
- [ ] **B.** Right-hand lane T-junction only
- [ ] **C.** Right-hand lane closed ahead
- [ ] **D.** 11 tonne weight limit

779 On a motorway this sign means

Mark one answer

- [ ] **A.** move over on to the hard shoulder
- [ ] **B.** overtaking on the left only
- [ ] **C.** leave the motorway at the next exit
- [ ] **D.** move to the lane on your left

780 What does '25' mean on this motorway sign?

Mark one answer

- [ ] **A.** The distance to the nearest town
- [ ] **B.** The route number of the road
- [ ] **C.** The number of the next junction
- [ ] **D.** The speed limit on the slip road

781 The right-hand lane of a three-lane motorway is

Mark one answer

- [ ] **A.** for lorries only
- [ ] **B.** an overtaking lane
- [ ] **C.** the right-turn lane
- [ ] **D.** an acceleration lane

782 Where can you find reflective amber studs on a motorway?

Mark one answer

- [ ] **A.** Separating the slip road from the motorway
- [ ] **B.** On the left-hand edge of the road
- [ ] **C.** On the right-hand edge of the road
- [ ] **D.** Separating the lanes

783 Where on a motorway would you find green reflective studs?

Mark one answer

- [ ] **A.** Separating driving lanes
- [ ] **B.** Between the hard shoulder and the carriageway
- [ ] **C.** At slip road entrances and exits
- [ ] **D.** Between the carriageway and the central reservation

784 You are travelling along a motorway. You see this sign. You should

Mark one answer

- [ ] **A.** leave the motorway at the next exit
- [ ] **B.** turn left immediately
- [ ] **C.** change lane
- [ ] **D.** move on to the hard shoulder

785 What does this sign mean?

Mark one answer

- [ ] **A.** No motor vehicles
- [ ] **B.** End of motorway
- [ ] **C.** No through road
- [ ] **D.** End of bus lane

786 Which of these signs means that the national speed limit applies?

Mark one answer

- [ ] A.

- [ ] B.

- [ ] C.

- [ ] D.

787 What is the maximum speed on a single carriageway road?

Mark one answer

- [ ] A. 50mph
- [ ] B. 60mph
- [ ] C. 40mph
- [ ] D. 70mph

788 What does this sign mean?

Mark one answer

- [ ] A. End of motorway
- [ ] B. End of restriction
- [ ] C. Lane ends ahead
- [ ] D. Free recovery ends

789 This sign is advising you to

Mark one answer

- [ ] A. follow the route diversion
- [ ] B. follow the signs to the picnic area
- [ ] C. give way to pedestrians
- [ ] D. give way to cyclists

790 Why would this temporary speed limit sign be shown?

Mark one answer

- [ ] A. To warn of the end of the motorway
- [ ] B. To warn you of a low bridge
- [ ] C. To warn you of a junction ahead
- [ ] D. To warn of road works ahead

791 This traffic sign means there is

Mark one answer

- [ ] A. a compulsory maximum speed limit
- [ ] B. an advisory maximum speed limit
- [ ] C. a compulsory minimum speed limit
- [ ] D. an advised separation distance

792 You see this sign at a crossroads. You should

Mark one answer

- ☐ **A.** maintain the same speed
- ☐ **B.** carry on with great care
- ☐ **C.** find another route
- ☐ **D.** telephone the police

793 You are signalling to turn right in busy traffic. How would you confirm your intention safely?

Mark one answer

- ☐ **A.** Sound the horn
- ☐ **B.** Give an arm signal
- ☐ **C.** Flash your headlights
- ☐ **D.** Position over the centre line

794 What does this sign mean?

Mark one answer

- ☐ **A.** Motorcycles only
- ☐ **B.** No cars
- ☐ **C.** Cars only
- ☐ **D.** No motorcycles

795 You are on a motorway. You see this sign on a lorry that has stopped in the right-hand lane. You should

Mark one answer

- ☐ **A.** move into the right-hand lane
- ☐ **B.** stop behind the flashing lights
- ☐ **C.** pass the lorry on the left
- ☐ **D.** leave the motorway at the next exit

796 You are on a motorway. Red flashing lights appear above your lane only. What should you do?

Mark one answer

- ☐ **A.** Continue in that lane and look for further information
- ☐ **B.** Move into another lane in good time
- ☐ **C.** Pull on to the hard shoulder
- ☐ **D.** Stop and wait for an instruction to proceed

797 A red traffic light means

Mark one answer

- ☐ **A.** you must stop behind the white stop line
- ☐ **B.** you may go straight on if there is no other traffic
- ☐ **C.** you may turn left if it is safe to do so
- ☐ **D.** you must slow down and prepare to stop if traffic has started to cross

798 The driver of this car is giving an arm signal. What are they about to do?

Mark one answer

- [ ] **A.** Turn to the right
- [ ] **B.** Turn to the left
- [ ] **C.** Go straight ahead
- [ ] **D.** Let pedestrians cross

799 Which arm signal tells you that the car you are following is going to turn left?

Mark one answer

- [ ] **A.**

- [ ] **B.**

- [ ] **C.**

- [ ] **D.**

800 When may you sound the horn?

Mark one answer

- [ ] **A.** To give you right of way
- [ ] **B.** To attract a friend's attention
- [ ] **C.** To warn others of your presence
- [ ] **D.** To make slower drivers move over

801 You must not use your horn when you are stationary

Mark one answer

- [ ] **A.** unless a moving vehicle may cause you danger
- [ ] **B.** at any time whatsoever
- [ ] **C.** unless it is used only briefly
- [ ] **D.** except for signalling that you have just arrived

802 What does this sign mean?

Mark one answer

- [ ] **A.** You can park on the days and times shown
- [ ] **B.** No parking on the days and times shown
- [ ] **C.** No parking at all from Monday to Friday
- [ ] **D.** End of the urban clearway restrictions

803 What does this sign mean?

Mark one answer

- [ ] **A.** Quayside or river bank
- [ ] **B.** Steep hill downwards
- [ ] **C.** Uneven road surface
- [ ] **D.** Road liable to flooding

804 You see this amber traffic light ahead. Which light or lights will come on next?

Mark one answer

- [ ] A. Red alone
- [ ] B. Red and amber together
- [ ] C. Green and amber together
- [ ] D. Green alone

805 This broken white line painted in the centre of the road means

Mark one answer

- [ ] A. oncoming vehicles have priority over you
- [ ] B. you should give priority to oncoming vehicles
- [ ] C. there is a hazard ahead of you
- [ ] D. the area is a national speed limit zone

806 Which sign means you have priority over oncoming vehicles?

Mark one answer

- [ ] A.

- [ ] B.

- [ ] C.

- [ ] D.

807 You see this signal overhead on the motorway. What does it mean?

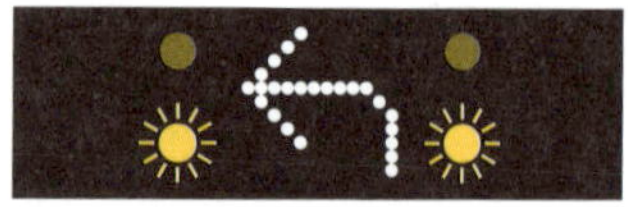

Mark one answer

- [ ] A. Leave the motorway at the next exit
- [ ] B. All vehicles use the hard shoulder
- [ ] C. Sharp bend to the left ahead
- [ ] D. Stop, all lanes ahead closed

808 A white line like this along the centre of the road is a

Mark one answer

- [ ] A. bus lane marking
- [ ] B. hazard warning
- [ ] C. give way marking
- [ ] D. lane marking

809 What is the purpose of these yellow criss-cross lines on the road?

Mark one answer

- [ ] **A.** To make you more aware of the traffic lights
- [ ] **B.** To guide you into position as you turn
- [ ] **C.** To prevent the junction becoming blocked
- [ ] **D.** To show you where to stop when the lights change

810 What is the reason for the yellow criss-cross lines painted on the road here?

Mark one answer

- [ ] **A.** To mark out an area for trams only
- [ ] **B.** To prevent queuing traffic from blocking the junction on the left
- [ ] **C.** To mark the entrance lane to a car park
- [ ] **D.** To warn you of the tram lines crossing the road

811 What is the reason for the area marked in red and white along the centre of this road?

Mark one answer

- [ ] **A.** It is to separate traffic flowing in opposite directions
- [ ] **B.** It marks an area to be used by overtaking motorcyclists
- [ ] **C.** It is a temporary marking to warn of the road works
- [ ] **D.** It is separating the two sides of the dual carriageway

812 Other drivers may sometimes flash their headlights at you. In which situation are they allowed to do this?

Mark one answer

- [ ] **A.** To warn of a radar speed trap ahead
- [ ] **B.** To show that they are giving way to you
- [ ] **C.** To warn you of their presence
- [ ] **D.** To let you know there is a fault with your vehicle

813 At road works which of the following can control traffic flow?

Mark three answers

- [ ] **A.** A STOP–GO board
- [ ] **B.** Flashing amber lights
- [ ] **C.** A police officer
- [ ] **D.** Flashing red lights
- [ ] **E.** Temporary traffic lights

814 You are approaching a zebra crossing where pedestrians are waiting. Which arm signal might you give?

Mark one answer

- [ ] **A.** 
- [ ] **B.** 
- [ ] **C.** 
- [ ] **D.** 

815 The white line along the side of the road

Mark one answer

- [ ] **A.** shows the edge of the carriageway
- [ ] **B.** shows the approach to a hazard
- [ ] **C.** means no parking
- [ ] **D.** means no overtaking

816 You see this white arrow on the road ahead. It means

Mark one answer

- [ ] **A.** entrance on the left
- [ ] **B.** all vehicles turn left
- [ ] **C.** keep left of the hatched markings
- [ ] **D.** road bending to the left

817 How should you give an arm signal to turn left?

Mark one answer

- [ ] **A.** 
- [ ] **B.** 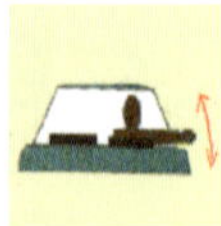
- [ ] **C.** 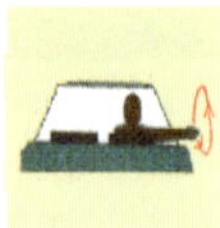
- [ ] **D.** 

818 You are waiting at a T-junction. A vehicle is coming from the right with the left signal flashing. What should you do?

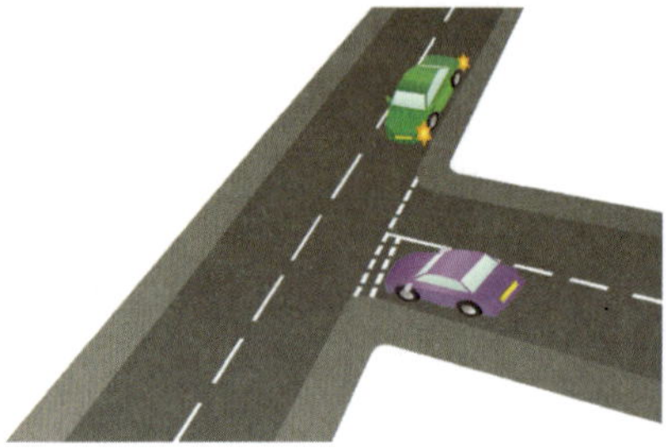

Mark one answer

- [ ] **A.** Move out and accelerate hard
- [ ] **B.** Wait until the vehicle starts to turn in
- [ ] **C.** Pull out before the vehicle reaches the junction
- [ ] **D.** Move out slowly

819 When may you use hazard warning lights when driving?

Mark one answer

- ☐ **A.** Instead of sounding the horn in a built-up area between 11.30pm and 7am
- ☐ **B.** On a motorway or unrestricted dual carriageway, to warn of a hazard ahead
- ☐ **C.** On rural routes, after a warning sign of animals
- ☐ **D.** On the approach to toucan crossings where cyclists are waiting to cross

820 You are driving on a motorway. There is a slow-moving vehicle ahead. On the back you see this sign. You should

Mark one answer

- ☐ **A.** pass on the right
- ☐ **B.** pass on the left
- ☐ **C.** leave at the next exit
- ☐ **D.** drive no further

821 In some narrow residential streets you may find a speed limit of

Mark one answer

- ☐ **A.** 20mph
- ☐ **B.** 25mph
- ☐ **C.** 35mph
- ☐ **D.** 40mph

822 You should NOT normally stop on these markings near schools

Mark one answer

- ☐ **A.** except when picking up children
- ☐ **B.** under any circumstances
- ☐ **C.** unless there is nowhere else available
- ☐ **D.** except to set down children

823 Why should you make sure that your indicators are cancelled after turning?

Mark one answer

- ☐ **A.** To avoid flattening the battery
- ☐ **B.** To avoid misleading other road users
- ☐ **C.** To avoid dazzling other road users
- ☐ **D.** To avoid damage to the indicator relay

824 You are driving in busy traffic. You want to pull up on the left just after a junction on the left. When should you signal?

Mark one answer

- ☐ **A.** As you are passing or just after the junction
- ☐ **B.** Just before you reach the junction
- ☐ **C.** Well before you reach the junction
- ☐ **D.** It would be better not to signal at all

825 An MOT certificate is normally valid for

Mark one answer

- [ ] **A.** three years after the date it was issued
- [ ] **B.** 10,000 miles
- [ ] **C.** one year after the date it was issued
- [ ] **D.** 30,000 miles

826 A cover note is a document issued before you receive your

Mark one answer

- [ ] **A.** driving licence
- [ ] **B.** insurance certificate
- [ ] **C.** registration document
- [ ] **D.** MOT certificate

827 A police officer asks to see your documents. You do not have them with you. You may produce them at a police station within

Mark one answer

- [ ] **A.** 5 days
- [ ] **B.** 7 days
- [ ] **C.** 14 days
- [ ] **D.** 21 days

828 You have just passed your practical test. You do not hold a full licence in another category. Within two years you get six penalty points on your licence. What will you have to do?

Mark two answers

- [ ] **A.** Retake only your theory test
- [ ] **B.** Retake your theory and practical tests
- [ ] **C.** Retake only your practical test
- [ ] **D.** Reapply for your full licence immediately
- [ ] **E.** Reapply for your provisional licence

829 To drive on the road learners MUST

Mark one answer

- [ ] **A.** have NO penalty points on their licence
- [ ] **B.** have taken professional instruction
- [ ] **C.** have a signed, valid provisional licence
- [ ] **D.** apply for a driving test within 12 months

830 Before driving anyone else's motor vehicle you should make sure that

Mark one answer

- [ ] **A.** the vehicle owner has third party insurance cover
- [ ] **B.** your own vehicle has insurance cover
- [ ] **C.** the vehicle is insured for your use
- [ ] **D.** the owner has left the insurance documents in the vehicle

831 Your car needs an MOT certificate. If you drive without one this could invalidate your

Mark one answer

- [ ] **A.** vehicle service record
- [ ] **B.** insurance
- [ ] **C.** road tax disc
- [ ] **D.** vehicle registration document

832 When is it legal to drive a car over three years old without an MOT certificate?

Mark one answer **NI**

- [ ] **A.** Up to seven days after the old certificate has run out
- [ ] **B.** When driving to an MOT centre to arrange an appointment
- [ ] **C.** Just after buying a second-hand car with no MOT
- [ ] **D.** When driving to an appointment at an MOT centre

833 To supervise a learner driver you must

Mark two answers

A. have held a full licence for at least 3 years
B. be at least 21 years old
C. be an approved driving instructor
D. hold an advanced driving certificate

834 How old must you be to supervise a learner driver?

Mark one answer

A. 18 years old
B. 19 years old
C. 20 years old
D. 21 years old

835 A newly qualified driver must

Mark one answer

A. display green 'L' plates
B. not exceed 40mph for 12 months
C. be accompanied on a motorway
D. have valid motor insurance

836 You have third party insurance. What does this cover?

Mark three answers

A. Damage to your own vehicle
B. Damage to your vehicle by fire
C. Injury to another person
D. Damage to someone's property
E. Damage to other vehicles
F. Injury to yourself

837 For which TWO of these must you show your motor insurance certificate?

Mark two answers

A. When you are taking your driving test
B. When buying or selling a vehicle
C. When a police officer asks you for it
D. When you are taxing your vehicle
E. When having an MOT inspection

838 Vehicle excise duty is often called 'Road Tax' or 'The Tax Disc'. You must

Mark one answer

A. keep it with your registration document
B. display it clearly on your vehicle
C. keep it concealed safely in your vehicle
D. carry it on you at all times

839 Motor cars must first have an MOT test certificate when they are

Mark one answer NI

A. one year old
B. three years old
C. five years old
D. seven years old

840 Your vehicle needs a current MOT certificate. You do not have one. Until you do have one you will not be able to renew your

Mark one answer

A. driving licence
B. vehicle insurance
C. road tax disc
D. vehicle registration document

841 Which THREE pieces of information are found on a vehicle registration document?

Mark three answers

A. Registered keeper
B. Make of the vehicle
C. Service history details
D. Date of the MOT
E. Type of insurance cover
F. Engine size

842 You have a duty to contact the licensing authority when

Mark three answers

- A. you go abroad on holiday
- B. you change your vehicle
- C. you change your name
- D. your job status is changed
- E. your permanent address changes
- F. your job involves travelling abroad

843 You must notify the licensing authority when

Mark three answers

- A. your health affects your driving
- B. your eyesight does not meet a set standard
- C. you intend lending your vehicle
- D. your vehicle requires an MOT certificate
- E. you change your vehicle

844 Your vehicle is insured third party only. This covers

Mark two answers

- A. damage to your vehicle
- B. damage to other vehicles
- C. injury to yourself
- D. injury to others
- E. all damage and injury

845 Your motor insurance policy has an excess of £100. What does this mean?

Mark one answer

- A. The insurance company will pay the first £100 of any claim
- B. You will be paid £100 if you do not have an accident
- C. Your vehicle is insured for a value of £100 if it is stolen
- D. You will have to pay the first £100 of any claim

846 When you apply to renew your vehicle excise licence (tax disc) you must produce

Mark one answer

- A. a valid insurance certificate
- B. the old tax disc
- C. the vehicle handbook
- D. a valid driving licence

847 What is the legal minimum insurance cover you must have to drive on public roads?

Mark one answer

- A. Third party, fire and theft
- B. Comprehensive
- C. Third party only
- D. Personal injury cover

848 Which THREE of the following do you need before you can drive legally?

Mark three answers

- A. A valid driving licence with signature
- B. A valid tax disc displayed on your vehicle
- C. A vehicle service record
- D. Proper insurance cover
- E. Breakdown cover
- F. A vehicle handbook

849 The cost of your insurance may reduce if you

Mark one answer **NI**

- A. are under 25 years old
- B. do not wear glasses
- C. pass the driving test first time
- D. take the Pass Plus scheme

850 Which of the following may reduce the cost of your insurance?

Mark one answer **NI**

- A. Having a valid MOT certificate
- B. Taking a Pass Plus course
- C. Driving a powerful car
- D. Having penalty points on your licence

851 The Pass Plus scheme has been created for new drivers. What is its main purpose?

NI

Mark one answer
- A. To allow you to drive faster
- B. To allow you to carry passengers
- C. To improve your basic skills
- D. To let you drive on motorways

852 How long will a Statutory Off Road Notification (SORN) last for?

Mark one answer
- A. 12 months
- B. 24 months
- C. 3 years
- D. 10 years

853 What is a Statutory Off Road Notification (SORN) declaration?

NI

Mark one answer
- A. A notification to tell VOSA that a vehicle does not have a current MOT
- B. Information kept by the police about the owner of the vehicle
- C. A notification to tell DVLA that a vehicle is not being used on the road
- D. Information held by insurance companies to check the vehicle is insured

854 A Statutory Off Road Notification (SORN) declaration is

NI

Mark one answer
- A. to tell DVLA that your vehicle is being used on the road but the MOT has expired
- B. to tell DVLA that you no longer own the vehicle
- C. to tell DVLA that your vehicle is not being used on the road
- D. to tell DVLA that you are buying a personal number plate

855 You claim on your insurance to have your car repaired. Your policy has an excess of £100. What does this mean?

Mark one answer
- A. The insurance company will pay the first £100 of any claim
- B. You will be paid £100 if you do not claim within one year
- C. Your vehicle is insured for a value of £100 if it is stolen
- D. You will have to pay the first £100 of the cost of repair to your car

856 A Statutory Off Road Notification (SORN) is valid

Mark one answer
- A. for as long as the vehicle has an MOT
- B. for 12 months only
- C. only if the vehicle is more than 3 years old
- D. provided the vehicle is insured

857 A Statutory Off Road Notification (SORN) will last

Mark one answer
- A. for the life of the vehicle
- B. for as long as you own the vehicle
- C. for 12 months only
- D.. until the vehicle warranty expires

858 What is the maximum specified fine for driving without insurance?

NI

Mark one answer
- A. £50
- B. £500
- C. £1000
- D. £5000

859 When should you update your Vehicle Registration Certificate (V5C)

Mark one answer

- A. When you pass your driving test
- B. When you move house
- C. When your vehicle needs an MOT
- D. When you have an accident

860 Who is legally responsible for ensuring that a Vehicle Registration Certificate (V5C) is updated?

Mark one answer

- A. The registered vehicle keeper
- B. The vehicle manufacturer
- C. Your insurance company
- D. The licensing authority

861 The Pass Plus scheme is designed to

Mark one answer NI

- A. give you a discount on your MOT
- B. improve your basic driving skills
- C. increase your mechanical knowledge
- D. allow you to drive anyone else's vehicle

862 By taking part in the Pass Plus scheme you will

Mark one answer NI

- A. never get any points on your licence
- B. be able to service your own car
- C. allow you to drive anyone else's vehicle
- D. improve your basic driving skills

863 **At the scene of an accident you should**

Mark one answer

- [ ] **A.** not put yourself at risk
- [ ] **B.** go to those casualties who are screaming
- [ ] **C.** pull everybody out of their vehicles
- [ ] **D.** leave vehicle engines switched on

864 **You are the first to arrive at the scene of an accident. Which FOUR of these should you do?**

Mark four answers

- [ ] **A.** Leave as soon as another motorist arrives
- [ ] **B.** Switch off the vehicle engine(s)
- [ ] **C.** Move uninjured people away from the vehicle(s)
- [ ] **D.** Call the emergency services
- [ ] **E.** Warn other traffic

865 **An accident has just happened. An injured person is lying in a busy road. What is the FIRST thing you should do to help?**

Mark one answer

- [ ] **A.** Treat the person for shock
- [ ] **B.** Warn other traffic
- [ ] **C.** Place them in the recovery position
- [ ] **D.** Make sure the injured person is kept warm

866 **You are the first person to arrive at an accident where people are badly injured. Which THREE should you do?**

Mark three answers

- [ ] **A.** Switch on your own hazard warning lights
- [ ] **B.** Make sure that someone telephones for an ambulance
- [ ] **C.** Try and get people who are injured to drink something
- [ ] **D.** Move the people who are injured clear of their vehicles
- [ ] **E.** Get people who are not injured clear of the scene

867 **You arrive at the scene of a motorcycle accident. The rider is injured. When should the helmet be removed?**

Mark one answer

- [ ] **A.** Only when it is essential
- [ ] **B.** Always straight away
- [ ] **C.** Only when the motorcyclist asks
- [ ] **D.** Always, unless they are in shock

868 **You arrive at a serious motorcycle accident. The motorcyclist is unconscious and bleeding. Your main priorities should be to**

Mark three answers

- [ ] **A.** try to stop the bleeding
- [ ] **B.** make a list of witnesses
- [ ] **C.** check the casualty's breathing
- [ ] **D.** take the numbers of the vehicles involved
- [ ] **E.** sweep up any loose debris
- [ ] **F.** check the casualty's airways

869 **You arrive at an accident. A motorcyclist is unconscious. Your FIRST priority is the casualty's**

Mark one answer

- [ ] **A.** breathing
- [ ] **B.** bleeding
- [ ] **C.** broken bones
- [ ] **D.** bruising

870 **At an accident a casualty is unconscious. Which THREE of the following should you check urgently?**

Mark three answers

- [ ] **A.** Circulation
- [ ] **B.** Airway
- [ ] **C.** Shock
- [ ] **D.** Breathing
- [ ] **E.** Broken bones

871 **You arrive at the scene of an accident. It has just happened and someone is unconscious. Which of the following should be given urgent priority to help them?**

Mark three answers

- A. Clear the airway and keep it open
- B. Try to get them to drink water
- C. Check that they are breathing
- D. Look for any witnesses
- E. Stop any heavy bleeding
- F. Take the numbers of vehicles involved

872 **At an accident someone is unconscious. Your main priorities should be to**

Mark three answers

- A. sweep up the broken glass
- B. take the names of witnesses
- C. count the number of vehicles involved
- D. check the airway is clear
- E. make sure they are breathing
- F. stop any heavy bleeding

873 **You have stopped at the scene of an accident to give help. Which THREE things should you do?**

Mark three answers

- A. Keep injured people warm and comfortable
- B. Keep injured people calm by talking to them reassuringly
- C. Keep injured people on the move by walking them around
- D. Give injured people a warm drink
- E. Make sure that injured people are not left alone

874 **You arrive at the scene of an accident. It has just happened and someone is injured. Which THREE of the following should be given urgent priority?**

Mark three answers

- A. Stop any severe bleeding
- B. Get them a warm drink
- C. Check that their breathing is OK
- D. Take numbers of vehicles involved
- E. Look for witnesses
- F. Clear their airway and keep it open

875 **At an accident a casualty has stopped breathing. You should**

Mark two answers

- A. remove anything that is blocking the mouth
- B. keep the head tilted forwards as far as possible
- C. raise the legs to help with circulation
- D. try to give the casualty something to drink
- E. tilt the head back gently to clear the airway

876 **You are at the scene of an accident. Someone is suffering from shock. You should**

Mark four answers

- A. reassure them constantly
- B. offer them a cigarette
- C. keep them warm
- D. avoid moving them if possible
- E. avoid leaving them alone
- F. give them a warm drink

877 **Which of the following should you NOT do at the scene of an accident?**

Mark one answer

- A. Warn other traffic by switching on your hazard warning lights
- B. Call the emergency services immediately
- C. Offer someone a cigarette to calm them down
- D. Ask drivers to switch off their engines

878 **There has been an accident. The driver is suffering from shock. You should**

Mark two answers

- **A.** give them a drink
- **B.** reassure them
- **C.** not leave them alone
- **D.** offer them a cigarette
- **E.** ask who caused the accident

879 **You have to treat someone for shock at the scene of an accident. You should**

Mark one answer

- **A.** reassure them constantly
- **B.** walk them around to calm them down
- **C.** give them something cold to drink
- **D.** cool them down as soon as possible

880 **You arrive at the scene of a motorcycle accident. No other vehicle is involved. The rider is unconscious, lying in the middle of the road. The first thing you should do is**

Mark one answer

- **A.** move the rider out of the road
- **B.** warn other traffic
- **C.** clear the road of debris
- **D.** give the rider reassurance

881 **At an accident a small child is not breathing. When giving mouth to mouth you should breathe**

Mark one answer

- **A.** sharply
- **B.** gently
- **C.** heavily
- **D.** rapidly

882 **To start mouth to mouth on a casualty you should**

Mark three answers

- **A.** tilt their head forward
- **B.** clear the airway
- **C.** turn them on their side
- **D.** tilt their head back gently
- **E.** pinch the nostrils together
- **F.** put their arms across their chest

883 **When you are giving mouth to mouth you should only stop when**

Mark one answer

- **A.** you think the casualty is dead
- **B.** the casualty can breathe without help
- **C.** the casualty has turned blue
- **D.** you think the ambulance is coming

884 **You arrive at the scene of an accident. There has been an engine fire and someone's hands and arms have been burnt. You should NOT**

Mark one answer

- **A.** douse the burn thoroughly with cool liquid
- **B.** lay the casualty down
- **C.** remove anything sticking to the burn
- **D.** reassure them constantly

885 **You arrive at an accident where someone is suffering from severe burns. You should**

Mark one answer

- **A.** apply lotions to the injury
- **B.** burst any blisters
- **C.** remove anything stuck to the burns
- **D.** douse the burns with cool liquid

886 **You arrive at the scene of an accident. A pedestrian has a severe bleeding wound on their leg, although it is not broken. What should you do?**

Mark two answers

- [ ] **A.** Dab the wound to stop bleeding
- [ ] **B.** Keep both legs flat on the ground
- [ ] **C.** Apply firm pressure to the wound
- [ ] **D.** Raise the leg to lessen bleeding
- [ ] **E.** Fetch them a warm drink

887 **You arrive at the scene of an accident. A passenger is bleeding badly from an arm wound. What should you do?**

Mark one answer

- [ ] **A.** Apply pressure over the wound and keep the arm down
- [ ] **B.** Dab the wound
- [ ] **C.** Get them a drink
- [ ] **D.** Apply pressure over the wound and raise the arm

888 **You arrive at the scene of an accident. A pedestrian is bleeding heavily from a leg wound but the leg is not broken. What should you do?**

Mark one answer

- [ ] **A.** Dab the wound to stop the bleeding
- [ ] **B.** Keep both legs flat on the ground
- [ ] **C.** Apply firm pressure to the wound
- [ ] **D.** Fetch them a warm drink

889 **At an accident a casualty is unconscious but still breathing. You should only move them if**

Mark one answer

- [ ] **A.** an ambulance is on its way
- [ ] **B.** bystanders advise you to
- [ ] **C.** there is further danger
- [ ] **D.** bystanders will help you to

890 **At an accident you suspect a casualty has back injuries. The area is safe. You should**

Mark one answer

- [ ] **A.** offer them a drink
- [ ] **B.** not move them
- [ ] **C.** raise their legs
- [ ] **D.** offer them a cigarette

891 **At an accident it is important to look after the casualty. When the area is safe, you should**

Mark one answer

- [ ] **A.** get them out of the vehicle
- [ ] **B.** give them a drink
- [ ] **C.** give them something to eat
- [ ] **D.** keep them in the vehicle

892 **A tanker is involved in an accident. Which sign would show that the tanker is carrying dangerous goods?**

Mark one answer

- [ ] **A.**

- [ ] **B.**

- [ ] **C.**

- [ ] **D.**

893 **The police may ask you to produce which three of these documents following an accident?**

Mark three answers

- [ ] **A.** Vehicle registration document
- [ ] **B.** Driving licence
- [ ] **C.** Theory test certificate
- [ ] **D.** Insurance certificate
- [ ] **E.** MOT test certificate
- [ ] **F.** Road tax disc

894 You see a car on the hard shoulder of a motorway with a HELP pennant displayed. This means the driver is most likely to be

Mark one answer

- [ ] **A.** a disabled person
- [ ] **B.** first aid trained
- [ ] **C.** a foreign visitor
- [ ] **D.** a rescue patrol person

895 On the motorway the hard shoulder should be used

Mark one answer

- [ ] **A.** to answer a mobile phone
- [ ] **B.** when an emergency arises
- [ ] **C.** for a short rest when tired
- [ ] **D.** to check a road atlas

896 For which TWO should you use hazard warning lights?

Mark two answers

- [ ] **A.** When you slow down quickly on a motorway because of a hazard ahead
- [ ] **B.** When you have broken down
- [ ] **C.** When you wish to stop on double yellow lines
- [ ] **D.** When you need to park on the pavement

897 When are you allowed to use hazard warning lights?

Mark one answer

- [ ] **A.** When stopped and temporarily obstructing traffic
- [ ] **B.** When travelling during darkness without headlights
- [ ] **C.** When parked for shopping on double yellow lines
- [ ] **D.** When travelling slowly because you are lost

898 You are on a motorway. A large box falls on to the road from a lorry. The lorry does not stop. You should

Mark one answer

- [ ] **A.** go to the next emergency telephone and inform the police
- [ ] **B.** catch up with the lorry and try to get the driver's attention
- [ ] **C.** stop close to the box until the police arrive
- [ ] **D.** pull over to the hard shoulder, then remove the box

899 There has been an accident. A motorcyclist is lying injured and unconscious. Unless it is essential, why should you usually not attempt to remove their helmet?

Mark one answer

- [ ] **A.** Because they may not want you to
- [ ] **B.** This could result in more serious injury
- [ ] **C.** They will get too cold if you do this
- [ ] **D.** Because you could scratch the helmet

900 After an accident, someone is unconscious in their vehicle. When should you call the emergency services?

Mark one answer

- [ ] **A.** Only as a last resort
- [ ] **B.** As soon as possible
- [ ] **C.** After you have woken them up
- [ ] **D.** After checking for broken bones

901 **An accident casualty has an injured arm. They can move it freely, but it is bleeding. Why should you get them to keep it in a raised position?**

Mark one answer
- [ ] **A.** Because it will ease the pain
- [ ] **B.** It will help them to be seen more easily
- [ ] **C.** To stop them touching other people
- [ ] **D.** It will help to reduce the bleeding

902 **You are going through a congested tunnel and have to stop. What should you do?**

Mark one answer
- [ ] **A.** Pull up very close to the vehicle in front to save space
- [ ] **B.** Ignore any message signs as they are never up to date
- [ ] **C.** Keep a safe distance from the vehicle in front
- [ ] **D.** Make a U-turn and find another route

903 **You are going through a tunnel. What should you look out for that warns of accidents or congestion?**

Mark one answer
- [ ] **A.** Hazard warning lines
- [ ] **B.** Other drivers flashing their lights
- [ ] **C.** Variable message signs
- [ ] **D.** Areas marked with hatch markings

904 **You are going through a tunnel. What systems are provided to warn of any accidents or congestion?**

Mark one answer
- [ ] **A.** Double white centre lines
- [ ] **B.** Variable message signs
- [ ] **C.** Chevron 'distance markers'
- [ ] **D.** Rumble strips

905 **While driving, a warning light on your vehicle's instrument panel comes on. You should**

Mark one answer
- [ ] **A.** continue if the engine sounds alright
- [ ] **B.** hope that it is just a temporary electrical fault
- [ ] **C.** deal with the problem when there is more time
- [ ] **D.** check out the problem quickly and safely

906 **You have broken down on a two-way road. You have a warning triangle. You should place the warning triangle at least how far from your vehicle?**

Mark one answer
- [ ] **A.** 5 metres (16 feet)
- [ ] **B.** 25 metres (82 feet)
- [ ] **C.** 45 metres (147 feet)
- [ ] **D.** 100 metres (328 feet)

907 **You break down on a level crossing. The lights have not yet begun to flash. Which THREE things should you do?**

Mark three answers
- [ ] **A.** Telephone the signal operator
- [ ] **B.** Leave your vehicle and get everyone clear
- [ ] **C.** Walk down the track and signal the next train
- [ ] **D.** Move the vehicle if a signal operator tells you to
- [ ] **E.** Tell drivers behind what has happened

908 Your vehicle has broken down on an automatic railway level crossing. What should you do FIRST?

Mark one answer

- [ ] **A.** Get everyone out of the vehicle and clear of the crossing
- [ ] **B.** Phone the signal operator so that trains can be stopped
- [ ] **C.** Walk along the track to give warning to any approaching trains
- [ ] **D.** Try to push the vehicle clear of the crossing as soon as possible

909 Your tyre bursts while you are driving. Which TWO things should you do?

Mark two answers

- [ ] **A.** Pull on the handbrake
- [ ] **B.** Brake as quickly as possible
- [ ] **C.** Pull up slowly at the side of the road
- [ ] **D.** Hold the steering wheel firmly to keep control
- [ ] **E.** Continue on at a normal speed

910 Which TWO things should you do when a front tyre bursts?

Mark two answers

- [ ] **A.** Apply the handbrake to stop the vehicle
- [ ] **B.** Brake firmly and quickly
- [ ] **C.** Let the vehicle roll to a stop
- [ ] **D.** Hold the steering wheel lightly
- [ ] **E.** Grip the steering wheel firmly

911 Your vehicle has a puncture on a motorway. What should you do?

Mark one answer

- [ ] **A.** Drive slowly to the next service area to get assistance
- [ ] **B.** Pull up on the hard shoulder. Change the wheel as quickly as possible
- [ ] **C.** Pull up on the hard shoulder. Use the emergency phone to get assistance
- [ ] **D.** Switch on your hazard lights. Stop in your lane

912 Which of these items should you carry in your vehicle for use in the event of an accident?

Mark three answers

- [ ] **A.** Road map
- [ ] **B.** Can of petrol
- [ ] **C.** Jump leads
- [ ] **D.** Fire extinguisher
- [ ] **E.** First aid kit
- [ ] **F.** Warning triangle

913 You are in an accident on a two-way road. You have a warning triangle with you. At what distance before the obstruction should you place the warning triangle?

Mark one answer

- [ ] **A.** 25 metres (82 feet)
- [ ] **B.** 45 metres (147 feet)
- [ ] **C.** 100 metres (328 feet)
- [ ] **D.** 150 metres (492 feet)

914 **You have broken down on a two-way road. You have a warning triangle. It should be displayed**

Mark one answer

- [ ] **A.** on the roof of your vehicle
- [ ] **B.** at least 150 metres (492 feet) behind your vehicle
- [ ] **C.** at least 45 metres (147 feet) behind your vehicle
- [ ] **D.** just behind your vehicle

915 **You have stalled in the middle of a level crossing and cannot restart the engine. The warning bell starts to ring. You should**

Mark one answer

- [ ] **A.** get out and clear of the crossing
- [ ] **B.** run down the track to warn the signal operator
- [ ] **C.** carry on trying to restart the engine
- [ ] **D.** push the vehicle clear of the crossing

916 **You are on the motorway. Luggage falls from your vehicle. What should you do?**

Mark one answer

- [ ] **A.** Stop at the next emergency telephone and contact the police
- [ ] **B.** Stop on the motorway and put on hazard lights while you pick it up
- [ ] **C.** Walk back up the motorway to pick it up
- [ ] **D.** Pull up on the hard shoulder and wave traffic down

917 **You are on a motorway. When can you use hazard warning lights?**

Mark two answers

- [ ] **A.** When a vehicle is following too closely
- [ ] **B.** When you slow down quickly because of danger ahead
- [ ] **C.** When you are towing another vehicle
- [ ] **D.** When driving on the hard shoulder
- [ ] **E.** When you have broken down on the hard shoulder

918 **You are involved in an accident with another vehicle. Someone is injured. Your vehicle is damaged. Which FOUR of the following should you find out?**

Mark four answers

- [ ] **A.** Whether the driver owns the other vehicle involved
- [ ] **B.** The other driver's name, address and telephone number
- [ ] **C.** The make and registration number of the other vehicle
- [ ] **D.** The occupation of the other driver
- [ ] **E.** The details of the other driver's vehicle insurance
- [ ] **F.** Whether the other driver is licensed to drive

919 **You have broken down on a motorway. When you use the emergency telephone you will be asked**

Mark three answers

- [ ] **A.** for the number on the telephone that you are using
- [ ] **B.** for your driving licence details
- [ ] **C.** for the name of your vehicle insurance company
- [ ] **D.** for details of yourself and your vehicle
- [ ] **E.** whether you belong to a motoring organisation

920 You lose control of your car and damage a garden wall. No one is around. What must you do?

NI

Mark one answer

- [ ] **A.** Report the accident to the police within 24 hours
- [ ] **B.** Go back to tell the house owner the next day
- [ ] **C.** Report the accident to your insurance company when you get home
- [ ] **D.** Find someone in the area to tell them about it immediately

921 Your engine catches fire. What should you do first?

Mark one answer

- [ ] **A.** Lift the bonnet and disconnect the battery
- [ ] **B.** Lift the bonnet and warn other traffic
- [ ] **C.** Call the breakdown service
- [ ] **D.** Call the fire brigade

922 Before driving through a tunnel what should you do?

Mark one answer

- [ ] **A.** Switch your radio off
- [ ] **B.** Remove any sunglasses
- [ ] **C.** Close your sunroof
- [ ] **D.** Switch on windscreen wipers

923 You are driving through a tunnel and the traffic is flowing normally. What should you do?

Mark one answer

- [ ] **A.** Use parking lights
- [ ] **B.** Use front spot lights
- [ ] **C.** Use dipped headlights
- [ ] **D.** Use rear fog lights

924 Before entering a tunnel it is good advice to

Mark one answer

- [ ] **A.** put on your sunglasses
- [ ] **B.** check tyre pressures
- [ ] **C.** change to a lower gear
- [ ] **D.** tune your radio to a local channel

925 You are driving through a tunnel. Your vehicle breaks down. What should you do?

Mark one answer

- [ ] **A.** Switch on hazard warning lights
- [ ] **B.** Remain in your vehicle
- [ ] **C.** Wait for the police to find you
- [ ] **D.** Rely on CCTV cameras seeing you

926 Your vehicle breaks down in a tunnel. What should you do?

Mark one answer

- [ ] **A.** Stay in your vehicle and wait for the police
- [ ] **B.** Stand in the lane behind your vehicle to warn others
- [ ] **C.** Stand in front of your vehicle to warn oncoming drivers
- [ ] **D.** Switch on hazard lights then go and call for help immediately

927 You have an accident while driving through a tunnel. You are not injured but your vehicle CANNOT be driven. What should you do first?

Mark one answer

- ☐ **A.** Rely on other drivers phoning for the police
- ☐ **B.** Switch off the engine and switch on hazard lights
- ☐ **C.** Take the names of witnesses and other drivers
- ☐ **D.** Sweep up any debris that is in the road

928 When driving through a tunnel you should

Mark one answer

- ☐ **A.** Look out for variable message signs
- ☐ **B.** Use your air conditioning system
- ☐ **C.** Switch on your rear fog lights
- ☐ **D.** Always use your windscreen wipers

929 What TWO safeguards could you take against fire risk to your vehicle?

Mark two answers

- ☐ **A.** Keep water levels above maximum
- ☐ **B.** Carry a fire extinguisher
- ☐ **C.** Avoid driving with a full tank of petrol
- ☐ **D.** Use unleaded petrol
- ☐ **E.** Check out any strong smell of petrol
- ☐ **F.** Use low octane fuel

930 Your vehicle catches fire while driving through a tunnel. It is still driveable. What should you do?

Mark one answer

- ☐ **A.** Leave it where it is with the engine running
- ☐ **B.** Pull up, then walk to an emergency telephone point
- ☐ **C.** Park it away from the carriageway
- ☐ **D.** Drive it out of the tunnel if you can do so

931 You are driving through a tunnel. Your vehicle catches fire. What should you do?

Mark one answer

- ☐ **A.** Continue through the tunnel if you can
- ☐ **B.** Turn your vehicle around immediately
- ☐ **C.** Reverse out of the tunnel
- ☐ **D.** Carry out an emergency stop

932 You are in a tunnel. Your vehicle is on fire and you CANNOT drive it. What should you do?

Mark two answers

- ☐ **A.** Stay in the vehicle and close the windows
- ☐ **B.** Switch on hazard warning lights
- ☐ **C.** Leave the engine running
- ☐ **D.** Try and put out the fire
- ☐ **E.** Switch off all of your lights
- ☐ **F.** Wait for other people to phone for help

933 You are driving through a tunnel. There has been an accident and the car in front is on fire and blocking the road. What should you do?

Mark one answer

- ☐ **A.** Overtake and continue as quickly as you can
- ☐ **B.** Lock all the doors and windows
- ☐ **C.** Switch on hazard warning lights
- ☐ **D.** Stop, then reverse out of the tunnel

934 You are towing a small trailer on a busy three-lane motorway. All the lanes are open. You must

Mark two answers

- [ ] **A.** not exceed 60mph
- [ ] **B.** not overtake
- [ ] **C.** have a stabiliser fitted
- [ ] **D.** use only the left and centre lanes

935 Any load that is carried on a roof rack should be

Mark one answer

- [ ] **A.** securely fastened when driving
- [ ] **B.** loaded towards the rear of the vehicle
- [ ] **C.** visible in your exterior mirror
- [ ] **D.** covered with plastic sheeting

936 You are planning to tow a caravan. Which of these will mostly help to aid the vehicle handling?

Mark one answer

- [ ] **A.** A jockey wheel fitted to the tow bar
- [ ] **B.** Power steering fitted to the towing vehicle
- [ ] **C.** Anti-lock brakes fitted to the towing vehicle
- [ ] **D.** A stabiliser fitted to the tow bar

937 If a trailer swerves or snakes when you are towing it you should

Mark one answer

- [ ] **A.** ease off the accelerator and reduce your speed
- [ ] **B.** let go of the steering wheel and let it correct itself
- [ ] **C.** brake hard and hold the pedal down
- [ ] **D.** increase your speed as quickly as possible

938 How can you stop a caravan snaking from side to side?

Mark one answer

- [ ] **A.** Turn the steering wheel slowly to each side
- [ ] **B.** Accelerate to increase your speed
- [ ] **C.** Stop as quickly as you can
- [ ] **D.** Slow down very gradually

939 On which TWO occasions might you inflate your tyres to more than the recommended normal pressure?

Mark two answers

- [ ] **A.** When the roads are slippery
- [ ] **B.** When driving fast for a long distance
- [ ] **C.** When the tyre tread is worn below 2mm
- [ ] **D.** When carrying a heavy load
- [ ] **E.** When the weather is cold
- [ ] **F.** When the vehicle is fitted with anti-lock brakes

940 A heavy load on your roof rack will

Mark one answer

- [ ] **A.** improve the road holding
- [ ] **B.** reduce the stopping distance
- [ ] **C.** make the steering lighter
- [ ] **D.** reduce stability

941 Are passengers allowed to ride in a caravan that is being towed?

Mark one answer

- [ ] **A.** Yes, if they are over 14
- [ ] **B.** No, not at any time
- [ ] **C.** Only if all the seats in the towing vehicle are full
- [ ] **D.** Only if a stabiliser is fitted

942
You are towing a caravan along a motorway. The caravan begins to swerve from side to side. What should you do?

Mark one answer
- [ ] **A.** Ease off the accelerator slowly
- [ ] **B.** Steer sharply from side to side
- [ ] **C.** Do an emergency stop
- [ ] **D.** Speed up very quickly

943
A trailer must stay securely hitched up to the towing vehicle. What additional safety device can be fitted to the trailer braking system?

Mark one answer
- [ ] **A.** Stabiliser
- [ ] **B.** Jockey wheel
- [ ] **C.** Corner steadies
- [ ] **D.** Breakaway cable

944
Overloading your vehicle can seriously affect the

Mark two answers
- [ ] **A.** gearbox
- [ ] **B.** steering
- [ ] **C.** handling
- [ ] **D.** battery life
- [ ] **E.** journey time

945
Who is responsible for making sure that a vehicle is not overloaded?

Mark one answer
- [ ] **A.** The driver of the vehicle
- [ ] **B.** The owner of the items being carried
- [ ] **C.** The person who loaded the vehicle
- [ ] **D.** The licensing authority

946
Which of these is a suitable restraint for a child under three years?

Mark one answer
- [ ] **A.** A child seat
- [ ] **B.** An adult holding a child
- [ ] **C.** An adult seat belt
- [ ] **D.** A lap belt

947
A child under three years is being carried in your vehicle. They should be secured in a restraint. Which of these is suitable?

Mark one answer
- [ ] **A.** An adult holding a child
- [ ] **B.** A lap belt
- [ ] **C.** A baby carrier
- [ ] **D.** An adult seat belt

948
Why would you fit a stabiliser before towing a caravan?

Mark one answer
- [ ] **A.** It will help with stability when driving in crosswinds
- [ ] **B.** It will allow heavy items to be loaded behind the axle
- [ ] **C.** It will help you to raise and lower the jockey wheel
- [ ] **D.** It will allow you to tow without the breakaway cable

949
You wish to tow a trailer. Where would you find the maximum noseweight of your vehicle's tow ball?

Mark one answer
- [ ] **A.** In the vehicle handbook
- [ ] **B.** In The Highway Code
- [ ] **C.** In your vehicle registration certificate
- [ ] **D.** In your licence documents

ALERTNESS – SECTION 1

1 C	2 BDF	3 C	4 D	5 C	6 C	7 C	8 C	9 B
10 D	11 AC	12 ABCD	13 AD	14 AB	15 AB	16 ABCD	17 C	18 B
19 D	20 B	21 C	22 B	23 B	24 ABE	25 C	26 B	27 B
28 D	29 C	30 C	31 C	32 A	33 D	34 D	35 B	36 A
37 D	38 B	39 B	40 B	41 B				

ATTITUDE – SECTION 2

42 D	43 A	44 C	45 B	46 C	47 D	48 D	49 B	50 B
51 BCD	52 ABE	53 A	54 D	55 B	56 A	57 A	58 B	59 A
60 A	61 C	62 A	63 B	64 D	65 D	66 D	67 A	68 A
69 B	70 C	71 A	72 C	73 A	74 C	75 B	76 C	77 DE
78 B	79 D	80 B	81 C	82 AB	83 D	84 C	85 A	86 A
87 B	88 A	89 D	90 C					

SAFETY AND YOUR VEHICLE – SECTION 3

91 B	92 AB	93 ABF	94 BEF	95 C	96 ACF	97 C	98 B	99 D
100 C	101 D	102 D	103 D	104 A	105 AE	106 D	107 B	108 D
109 D	110 A	111 B	112 BCDF	113 D	114 D	115 BC	116 BC	117 A
118 D	119 A	120 B	121 B	122 D	123 C	124 D	125 D	126 D
127 B	128 B	129 B	130 D	131 ABF	132 ABC	133 ABC	134 BDF	135 ADE
136 BD	137 B	138 CDE	139 B	140 B	141 C	142 B	143 DE	144 A
145 C	146 B	147 D	148 D	149 D	150 B	151 C	152 A	153 B
154 D	155 A	156 C	157 A	158 B	159 AB	160 A	161 D	162 B
163 BCD	164 C	165 CD	166 A	167 A	168 D	169 C	170 B	171 B
172 B	173 D	174 ABE	175 ADE	176 D	177 A	178 B	179 C	180 D
181 A	182 B	183 C	184 D	185 A	186 C	187 D	188 B	189 B
190 A	191 A	192 B	193 D	194 B	195 A	196 C	197 D	198 B
199 B								

SAFETY MARGINS – SECTION 4

200 D	201 D	202 BC	203 B	204 D	205 D	206 C	207 C	208 A
209 ACE	210 B	211 A	212 B	213 A	214 B	215 AE	216 C	217 B
218 C	219 BDEF	220 B	221 D	222 A	223 C	224 A	225 AD	226 C
227 B	228 B	229 B	230 C	231 C	232 B	233 B	234 BC	235 C
236 C	237 B	238 C	239 D	240 BC	241 B	242 ACE	243 D	244 D
245 D	246 A	247 D	248 BD	249 D	250 B	251 A	252 D	253 A
254 B	255 B							

HAZARD AWARENESS – SECTION 5

256 D	257 CD	258 B	259 C	260 A	261 D	262 ACE	263 D	264 C
265 A	266 C	267 C	268 D	269 B	270 B	271 A	272 A	273 A
274 C	275 C	276 CD	277 A	278 B	279 A	280 C	281 BF	282 B
283 AE	284 A	285 D	286 D	287 C	288 B	289 B	290 C	291 A
292 B	293 B	294 CD	295 B	296 D	297 B	298 A	299 A	300 D
301 A	302 B	303 AE	304 C	305 B	306 BC	307 D	308 B	309 B
310 C	311 D	312 C	313 CD	314 AC	315 AB	316 A	317 A	318 B
319 A	320 ABC	321 C	322 C	323 C	324 ABE	325 C	326 D	327 D
328 C	329 C	330 D	331 ABD	332 ABC	333 D	334 C	335 AB	336 B
337 B	338 CD	339 D	340 ACE	341 ABE	342 A	343 A	344 D	345 D
346 A	347 D	348 A	349 A	350 ACD	351 B	352 B		

VULNERABLE ROAD USERS – SECTION 6

353 D	354 D	355 C	356 C	357 B	358 D	359 D	360 AD	361 B
362 C	363 D	364 A	365 D	366 D	367 B	368 D	369 B	370 D
371 D	372 C	373 AC	374 C	375 C	376 A	377 D	378 C	379 D
380 ABC	381 C	382 B	383 B	384 AC	385 ABD	386 B	387 D	388 A
389 A	390 D	391 D	392 A	393 A	394 C	395 C	396 C	397 D
398 ACE	399 D	400 B	401 A	402 C	403 D	404 C	405 C	406 A
407 D	408 D	409 A	410 A	411 B	412 B	413 D	414 C	415 C
416 B	417 C	418 AE	419 D	420 C	421 C	422 B	423 B	424 D
425 D	426 A	427 C	428 C	429 D	430 D	431 B	432 A	433 D
434 B	435 B	436 C						

OTHER TYPES OF VEHICLE – SECTION 7

437 A	438 A	439 B	440 B	441 D	442 B	443 A	444 BC	445 B
446 D	447 A	448 A	449 C	450 B	451 D	452 D	453 D	454 B
455 B	456 B	457 AC	458 BD	459 B	460 D	461 D	462 A	463 A

VEHICLE HANDLING – SECTION 8

464 ACE	465 A	466 CD	467 D	468 A	469 BDF	470 C	471 D	472 C
473 DE	474 D	475 B	476 C	477 C	478 D	479 D	480 D	481 C
482 C	483 BD	484 BD	485 D	486 B	487 C	488 CE	489 C	490 D
491 A	492 A	493 C	494 B	495 ABDF	496 A	497 D	498 B	499 B
500 AB	501 BD	502 A	503 ACD	504 B	505 A	506 C	507 B	508 A
509 A	510 C	511 C	512 A	513 B	514 C	515 D	516 B	517 D
518 ABD	519 D	520 C	521 C	522 C	523 D	524 D	525 A	526 B

MOTORWAY RULES – SECTION 9

527 ADEF	528 ADEF	529 D	530 D	531 D	532 D	533 A	534 B	535 C
536 BE	537 C	538 A	539 C	540 A	541 D	542 A	543 C	544 C
545 C	546 C	547 C	548 C	549 B	550 C	551 B	552 B	553 A
554 B	555 B	556 D	557 CDF	558 C	559 D	560 C	561 D	562 A
563 B	564 B	565 D	566 C	567 A	568 B	569 D	570 A	571 D
572 D	573 A	574 C	575 B	576 B	577 C	578 A	579 A	580 B
581 D	582 D	583 B	584 D	585 D	586 B	587 C	588 D	589 D
590 C	591 A	592 D						

RULES OF THE ROAD – SECTION 10

593 C	594 C	595 D	596 B	597 A	598 C	599 D	600 ADF	601 AD
602 A	603 B	604 A	605 B	606 A	607 D	608 A	609 D	610 D
611 C	612 A	613 ACE	614 B	615 C	616 D	617 BD	618 B	619 A
620 D	621 C	622 A	623 B	624 CDE	625 B	626 AE	627 B	628 A
629 ABD	630 A	631 B	632 B	633 A	634 D	635 A	636 D	637 C
638 D	639 D	640 BEF	641 D	642 D	643 D	644 C	645 C	646 D
647 A	648 A	649 A	650 C	651 B	652 A	653 D	654 AB	655 A
656 D	657 D	658 A	659 D	660 B	661 ABC	662 D	663 A	664 D
665 A	666 A	667 B	668 C					

ROAD AND TRAFFIC SIGNS – SECTION 11

669 D	670 D	671 A	672 A	673 B	674 A	675 D	676 B	677 D
678 D	679 D	680 A	681 C	682 B	683 D	684 C	685 B	686 A
687 B	688 B	689 C	690 C	691 A	692 C	693 B	694 C	695 B
696 D	697 D	698 C	699 D	700 C	701 B	702 C	703 D	704 A
705 D	706 B	707 D	708 B	709 A	710 A	711 A	712 A	713 B
714 B	715 A	716 D	717 ACEF	718 C	719 A	720 A	721 C	722 D
723 B	724 C	725 B	726 B	727 B	728 B	729 D	730 A	731 C
732 A	733 C	734 D	735 A	736 C	737 B	738 D	739 A	740 B
741 B	742 C	743 C	744 A	745 A	746 C	747 C	748 B	749 D
750 C	751 B	752 A	753 C	754 D	755 C	756 B	757 A	758 A
759 C	760 BDF	761 A	762 C	763 C	764 B	765 B	766 A	767 C
768 A	769 B	770 A	771 B	772 D	773 D	774 B	775 A	776 A
777 D	778 C	779 D	780 C	781 B	782 C	783 C	784 A	785 B
786 D	787 B	788 B	789 A	790 D	791 A	792 B	793 B	794 D
795 C	796 B	797 A	798 B	799 A	800 C	801 A	802 B	803 A
804 A	805 C	806 C	807 A	808 B	809 C	810 B	811 A	812 C
813 ACE	814 A	815 A	816 C	817 C	818 B	819 B	820 B	821 A
822 B	823 B	824 A						

Answers to Questions – Section 15

DOCUMENTS – SECTION 12

825 C	826 B	827 B	828 BE	829 C	830 C	831 B	832 D	833 AB
834 D	835 D	836 CDE	837 CD	838 B	839 B	840 C	841 ABF	842 BCE
843 ABE	844 BD	845 D	846 A	847 C	848 ABD	849 D	850 B	851 C
852 A	853 C	854 C	855 D	856 B	857 C	858 D	859 B	860 A
861 B	862 D							

ACCIDENTS – SECTION 13

863 A	864 BCDE	865 B	866 ABE	867 A	868 ACF	869 A	870 ABD	871 ACE
872 DEF	873 ABE	874 ACF	875 AE	876 ACDE	877 C	878 BC	879 A	880 B
881 B	882 BDE	883 B	884 C	885 D	886 CD	887 D	888 C	889 C
890 B	891 D	892 B	893 BDE	894 A	895 B	896 AB	897 A	898 A
899 B	900 B	901 D	902 C	903 C	904 B	905 D	906 C	907 ABD
908 A	909 CD	910 CE	911 C	912 DEF	913 B	914 C	915 A	916 A
917 BE	918 ABCE	919 ADE	920 A	921 D	922 B	923 C	924 D	925 A
926 D	927 B	928 A	929 BE	930 D	931 A	932 BD	933 C	

VEHICLE LOADING – SECTION 14

934 AD	935 A	936 D	937 A	938 D	939 BD	940 D	941 B	942 A
943 D	944 BC	945 A	946 A	947 C	948 A	949 A		